Sorting out the truth about safe foods
can be difficult. . . .

- Some doctors say to eat fish several times a week—
  others warn of mercury and PCB contamination.

- Researchers in a recent study expressed concern about
  the arsenic in chicken. Should you and your children
  pass on the chicken wings?

- Of more than 140 million pounds of meat recalled because of contamination, less than 30 percent was ever
  recovered. How do you know if the meat in your refrigerator has been recalled?

- You know you should eat at least five servings of fruits
  and vegetables a day, but what about pesticides?

. . . but not with

Safe Foods

*The A-to-Z Guide to the Most Wholesome
Foods for You and Your Family*

SAFE FOODS

The A-to-Z Guide to the Most
Wholesome Foods for You and
Your Family

Deborah Mitchell

A SIGNET BOOK

SIGNET
Published by New American Library, a division of
Penguin Group (USA) Inc., 375 Hudson Street,
New York, New York 10014, USA
Penguin Group (Canada), 10 Alcorn Avenue, Toronto,
Ontario M4V 3B2, Canada (a division of Pearson Penguin Canada Inc.)
Penguin Books Ltd., 80 Strand, London WC2R 0RL, England
Penguin Ireland, 25 St. Stephen's Green, Dublin 2,
Ireland (a division of Penguin Books Ltd.)
Penguin Group (Australia), 250 Camberwell Road, Camberwell, Victoria 3124,
Australia (a division of Pearson Australia Group Pty. Ltd.)
Penguin Books India Pvt. Ltd., 11 Community Centre, Panchsheel Park,
New Delhi - 110 017, India
Penguin Group (NZ), Cnr Airborne and Rosedale Roads, Albany,
Auckland 1310, New Zealand (a division of Pearson New Zealand Ltd.)
Penguin Books (South Africa) (Pty.) Ltd., 24 Sturdee Avenue,
Rosebank, Johannesburg 2196, South Africa

Penguin Books Ltd., Registered Offices:
80 Strand, London WC2R 0RL, England

First published by Signet, an imprint of New American Library,
a division of Penguin Group (USA) Inc.

First Printing, October 2004
10 9 8 7 6 5 4 3 2 1

PUBLISHER'S NOTE
Every effort as been made to ensure that the information contained in this book is
complete and accurate. However, neither the publisher nor the author is engaged
in rendering professional advice or services to the individual reader. The ideas, proce-
dures, and suggestions contained in this book are not intended as a substitute for
consulting with your physician. All matters regarding your health require medical
supervision. Neither the author nor the publisher shall be liable or responsible for
any loss or damage allegedly arising from any information or suggestion in this book.

Contents

Introduction

Three or more times a day, you have a unique opportunity: to provide your children and yourself with foods that can enhance your health, improve your mood, boost your energy, and give you a sense of well-being. Because you care about your family, you want your food choices not only to taste good, but also to be safe, as free as possible of potentially dangerous ingredients or contaminants that may pose a special risk to your children's health and your own.

This book will help you make those choices, by showing you which foods are safest and most beneficial for your family, where you can get those foods, the best ways to prepare and store them, and how to identify sources of potentially harmful ingredients or contaminants. You can take this book with you to the supermarket so you can make decisions on the spot about whether a specific product is a healthy choice for your family.

If you are like many consumers, you are puzzled by the confusing, sometimes contradictory claims made by food producers, government agencies, consumer groups, and research firms about the safety and nutritional value of America's food supply. Are organic fruits and vegetables a better choice for your family, and are they worth the extra expense in the long run? If irradiating meat is supposed to be safe, why have so many other countries banned it? What do experts *really* know about the safety of genetically engineered foods? How concerned should you be about the hormones, pesticides, and antibiotics that are in the meats and dairy products your children eat? You're told to eat fish several times a week, but should you worry about mercury contamination?

We have combed the mountains of research material on these and other food safety issues, sorted it out, and created an easy-to-follow guide to the safest and least safe foods in each of eight categories: fruits and vegetables, grains and cereals, nuts and legumes, meat, poultry, fish, dairy and eggs, and oils and fats. In *Safe Foods*, you have an effective, powerful tool to help ensure your family is buying and eating the healthiest food possible. You will learn:

- **Additives:** Which food additives are deemed to be safe and which ones should concern you most and why, and how to avoid them.
- **Pesticides:** That more than 400 different pesticides are used on food crops, which of them are safe, and how you can protect your family against any ill effects they may cause.
- **Irradiation:** How irradiation may or may not affect your family's health.
- **Genetically engineered foods:** What experts know and don't know about genetically engineered foods and how to use this information to make an informed choice when buying for your family.
- **Hormones and antibiotics:** Which foods are the largest reservoirs for hormones (including steroids) and antibiotics and how to avoid them.
- **Food pathogens:** How to avoid foodborne pathogens, which cause an estimated 33 million to nearly 100 million illnesses per year.
- **Storage and preparation:** How to store and prepare your food purchases for maximum nutritional value and safety.

You will discover how to make better informed food choices when you get the answers to these and other questions about foods in the following categories:

- **Fruits and Vegetables:** What are the best and worst choices in each category? What are the differences between organically and conventionally grown produce?
- **Grains and Cereals:** Enriched, fortified, bleached, natural, organic, genetically engineered—does it matter which you choose for your family?
- **Meat and Poultry:** Conventionally raised, organically produced, hormone-free or free-range—what impact do your choices have on your health?
- **Eggs and Dairy:** Free-range, hormone-free, organic, low-fat, fat-free—what do these terms mean and how can you use the information to make informed purchases?
- **Fish:** When should you be concerned about mercury and other contaminants in fish? What are the advantages and disadvantages of eating fish raised on fish farms?
- **Trans Fats:** What's the scoop on these cholesterol-elevating fats that are found in so many popular processed foods? Are they safe for your children?

Is Your Child's Health at Risk?

Everyone who eats needs to read *Safe Foods*, but especially pregnant women and parents of young children. Why? Pesticides, pathogens, and other food contaminants can harm young, vulnerable bodies more than those of older children and adults.

Mothers-to-be are responsible for the most vulnerable lives. A developing fetus is very sensitive to contaminants that can reach it through the placenta, not only because many of these substances are toxic, but also because a fetus does not have all the defenses it needs to protect itself against these invaders.

Pound for pound, young children eat more dairy, meat, and eggs than older people. They also eat more foods that are high in pesticide residues, such as fresh fruits and vegetables and juices. The typical one-year-old child eats up to seven times more carrots, broccoli, grapes, and pears than the average adult.

How can you help provide your children with food that nurtures their growing bodies and minds while protecting your health as well?

Safe Foods shows you how. Given the dizzying number of food products on the market and the hectic lifestyles of most people, this book is a convenient, comprehensive, and much needed guide for individuals who want to cut through the confusion and find safe, healthy foods for themselves and their family. It's not about giving up favorite foods; it's about making informed choices and, in some cases, introducing new foods into your life.

PART I

The Changing Face of American Food

CHAPTER 1

Playing with Your Food

Once upon a time you could walk into an orchard, pick an apple off a tree, shine it against your sleeve until it glowed, and eat it without fear of ingesting pesticides, herbicides, fungicides, or wax used to make the skin shiny and appealing. Short of finding a worm inside the apple, you were ensured a healthy treat.

Once upon a time you could cast your net into the ocean or a river, haul in sea bass or salmon, and be ensured a pesticide-free, mercury-free fish dinner.

Once upon a time you could pluck a ripe, juicy tomato from the vine and take a bite without wondering whether it had been genetically modified and possibly contained fish genes to help improve its shelf life.

Once upon a time foods such as ice cream, bread, cakes, cookies, and pies were made with wholesome, natural ingredients, and you didn't need a chemistry degree to pronounce and decipher the names of the preservatives, artificial colors and flavors, and fillers in these foods.

That was once upon a time. Today, hundreds of thousands of people handle or make modifications to your food before it reaches your table. These people include government employees, scientists, farmers, slaughterhouse workers, pesticide sprayers, feedlot operators, canning facility workers, food inspectors, truckers, grocers, and many others who have a hand in the quality and safety of the food you eat. Unless you grow or produce all of your own food, you entrust the quality and safety of your food—and thus your health—to these individuals every day.

Let's take a look at some of the organizations and people who play a critical role in determining and maintaining the quality of your food.

WHO'S WATCHING OVER YOUR FOOD?

Because so many people have their hands on your food before it even reaches your table, it's good to know that there are many organizations—both public and private—working to ensure food safety and quality. We gathered much of the information in this book from these organizations, as well as from current research studies. Throughout this book you will see the following organizations, among others, mentioned:

- Environmental Protection Agency (EPA): Determines the pesticide residue levels that may legally remain on food. These levels are called "tolerances" and are monitored by another government agency, the Food and Drug Administration (FDA).
- Food and Drug Administration (FDA): Monitors both domestic and imported foods to make sure pesticide tolerances set by the EPA are not exceeded. One way it does this is through the Total Diet Study, a yearly program in which more than 286 types of food are analyzed for levels of pesticides as well as industrial chemicals and various elements (e.g., lead, mercury, zinc). You will read more about this study, its results, and what you can do to help avoid these food contaminants in Part II of this book. The FDA also sets tolerances for drug residues in raw meat, poultry, milk, and eggs.
- United States Department of Agriculture (USDA): Has several programs that monitor food safety: for

example, the Pesticide Data Program, which checks pesticide levels in a limited number of samples of fruits and vegetables, rice, beef, poultry, and water each year, and the Food Safety Inspection Service, which measures, for example, the levels of arsenic in chicken.

- Agency for Toxic Substances and Disease Registry: Agency of the US Department of Health and Human Services that advises the EPA on hazardous waste sites and spills, provides health information to prevent harmful exposures and disease related to toxic substances, and determines the level of public health hazards at waste sites.
- Natural Resource Defense Council: Nonprofit organization of scientists, environmental specialists, and lawyers, dedicated to protecting public health and the environment; provides a wealth of information on these topics to the public.
- Consumers Union of the United States: An advocacy group that helps consumers reduce their exposure to pesticides and farmers reduce their use of pesticides.
- Environmental Working Group: A nonprofit organization that reports on the use of pesticides in food.

Despite the well-intentioned efforts of these and other organizations and individuals, America's food supply is not one hundred percent safe. If it were, up to an estimated 100 million people each year wouldn't get food poisoning; tens of thousands of people might not get cancer; an unknown number of people might not experience miscarriages, impaired fertility, immune system diseases, and behavioral or neurological problems. The list, unfortunately, could go on and on.

The truth is, although researchers and other experts are constantly evaluating pesticides, food additives, and other substances in our food, no one knows for certain what impact chronic exposure may have on our health. Pesticide tolerances the EPA determined to be safe years ago may be found to be harmful in the future. Drug

levels the FDA once said were safe may reveal themselves to have serious negative effects in years to come.

Even seemingly innocuous substances can be found to
be harmful. In the early part of the new millennium,
experts finally decided, after years of studies, that the
trans fats found in hydrogenated and partially hydrogenated oils, which have been used for decades in many
processed foods and in margarines, posed a significant
health risk. Thus by January 2006, food manufacturers
are required to list the trans fat content on their labels.
Although trans fats were not banned, this situation dem-
onstrates how a substance that is found in virtually everyone's diet was allowed, unknowingly, to remain there
without even a warning.

HOW OTHERS PLAY WITH YOUR FOOD

It's safe to say that virtually everyone in the United
States depends on commercially produced food to feed
themselves and their family. Naturally some people have
their own gardens, raise their own chickens, milk their
own cows, or slaughter their own livestock. Even the
most self-sufficient, however, still depend, at least occasionally, on commercial products, products that typically
go through many hands before reaching the kitchen
table.

Food is manipulated in three ways: through behind-
the-scenes regulations (government and industry), intentional manipulation, and unintentional manipulation. All
of these methods are complicated, but we will give you
some highlights so you'll have a better understanding
of how others played with the dinner that sits before
you tonight.

Government and Industry Manipulation

In 1862, the United States Department of Agriculture
(USDA) was created and assigned two tasks: to ensure
that Americans had an adequate and reliable supply of

food, and to help educate Americans about agriculture, nutrition, and food. As the population of the United States grew and the demand for food followed suit, these tasks became more difficult to achieve. At the same time, innovations were being introduced in how food was produced, preserved, and packaged.

One striking introduction occurred around the turn of the century, when margarine and hydrogenated oils burst onto the scene. For years, there were heated arguments between the dairy industry and margarine advocates, as the former was afraid it would lose its hold on the market. Those disputes were eventually settled, and today, about a hundred years later, we now find ourselves engaged in another debate, this time over how hydrogenated and partially hydrogenated oils, which contain trans fats (discussed in chapter 14), can harm our health. And once again, various sectors of the food industry are worried about their bottom line.

Although the USDA originally seemed to be a consumer-friendly organization, over the years it has repeatedly caved in to the demands and protests of many food and food-related industry representatives (e.g., cattle ranchers, dairy industry, pesticide manufacturers, sugar producers, egg producers) over issues that could hurt their profits.

"Diet is a political issue," says Marion Nestle, author of *Food Politics* and professor and chair of the Department of Nutrition and Food Studies at New York University. And where there's politics there's fire. Thus food is also a highly charged issue, as is food safety. Any person, group, or industry that gives advice on how Americans should make food choices will ultimately affect food sales; therefore, individuals or companies that have a vested interest in food or food production will not take kindly to any efforts that have a negative impact on their sales and thus profits. Because the various food companies command hundreds of billions of dollars (the largest food producers in the United States generate more than $30 billion in sales annually), they wield tremendous political power when they demand favorable (translated, "cost-effective" and "profitable") regulations for their industry.

Example of Government and Industry Manipulation.
Let's take a brief look at the politics behind food safety. A good place to start is with lobbyists. Lobbyists are individuals who are hired (not elected) and paid to represent the private interests of, say, pesticide manufacturers, snack food producers, soda makers, cattle ranchers, food additive suppliers, and apple growers. The Center for Responsive Politics estimates that food and agriculture lobbyists spent $52 million in 1998 to persuade lawmakers on food issues other than tobacco. And you can be sure that the lobbyists are fighting for issues that will help keep a healthy bottom line for their respective industries.

Here's just one example out of thousands of how lobbyists work. When the USDA and the DHHS (Department of Health and Human Services, a government agency that influences nutrition education and research) appointed an advisory committee to revise the Food Pyramid for 2000, sugar was a hotly debated issue. The sugar industry argued that there was insufficient evidence linking sugar and disease and thus people should not be encouraged to eat less sugar. This argument was made despite the fact that sugar has no nutritional value and that it has been linked with obesity (a growing problem in children, who consume large amounts of sugar), tooth decay, diabetes, and other health problems.

Lobbyists for the sugar industry fought to make the wording of the guidelines as ambiguous and as "sugar-friendly" as possible for consumers. In February 2000, the advisory committee suggested the wording "choose beverages and foods that limit your intake of sugars." The word "limit" angered the sugar lobbyists, who considered it a threat to the $26 billion sugar industry. The lobbyists then hounded thirty senators, half of whom were from states that produced sugar, to "question whether the USDA had the right to 'change the sugar guidelines based on existing science.'" There were even protests from the Grocery Manufacturers of America, which said that the "minimum burden of scientific proof has not been met" to encourage people to limit their intake of sugar.

So what did the guidelines on sugar finally say? "Choose beverages and foods to moderate your intake of sugars." In other words, consumers were given no guidance at all.

That's not to say that every decision that comes down from the USDA (or the FDA and EPA) doesn't benefit food safety and your health. However, many of the regulations that are passed raise more questions and concerns than they answer. We will explore some of these issues in later chapters, specifically when we discuss organically produced versus conventionally produced food and how pesticides affect your health and that of your children; irradiated food; genetically modified food; and the use of food additives.

Should you, as a consumer, be concerned about how government and industry manipulate your food? We think better words than "concerned" are aware, vigilant, educated, and proactive. This book will help you be all four.

Intentional Manipulation

Intentional physical manipulation of food includes changes that food scientists, producers, and processors make to food products. More people are familiar with this category because it gets more press than the behind-the-scenes manipulations of government, food, and pesticide industry representatives. Intentional manipulation includes the following:

- Use of pesticides, herbicides, insecticides, fungicides, and rodenticides
- Genetically modified food
- Irradiation
- Use of food additives

- Food preservation, including drying, heating, freezing, fermentation, and the addition of chemicals

We'll take a brief look at each of these approaches, and then discuss them in more detail in chapters 2 through 5.

Pesticides, Herbicides, Insecticides, Fungicides, and Rodenticides. A huge controversy surrounds the use of pesticides and other potentially dangerous substances that are applied to food crops to control or eliminate pests and diseases. Use of these products is synonymous with conventional farming; thus it raises the question of whether organically produced food (which does not use these substances) is safer, healthier, and more environmentally friendly than conventionally produced food.

On the one hand, many farmers and farm organizations (e.g., the American Farm Bureau Federation) say they need to use pesticides because they are relatively inexpensive, they provide good control of insect and plant pests, and thus they help farmers stay in business. Pesticide manufacturers have a natural interest in keeping their products on the market, as well as introducing new ones.

On the other hand, advocates of organic foods are worried about the health hazards associated with pesticides (especially for children) and the negative impact on the environment. They emphasize that even though the amount of pesticide residue on many fruits, vegetables, and grains, and in meats, dairy products, and poultry are below hazardous levels (according to US government agencies and some nongovernmental organizations), and while a few exposures to pesticides in food are probably not harmful, *it's the cumulative effects of these poisons that are of concern.* Everyone has to eat, and so we are exposed to pesticides several times a day, every day of our lives. In addition to being in our food, pesticides are all around us: in office buildings, furniture, lawns, parks, airplanes, schools, and water. And although

we are exposed to pesticides in so many ways, we have
the power to significantly limit our exposure from those
in food. We talk more about pesticides and related substances in chapters 2 and 3, and in Part II we will help
you choose foods that will reduce your exposure to them.

Food Additives. Preservatives. Artificial colors. Artificial flavors. Stabilizers. Fillers. These and other substances fall into the category of "food additives,"
ingredients that are intentionally added to food to improve or enhance flavor, form, texture, shelf life, or color.
Examples of food additives are hormones injected into
cows to increase milk production, ascorbic acid (which
adds color), and calcium disodium EDTA, which helps
promote color retention. This category does *not* include
substances that unintentionally get into food items, such
as those that may seep into food from packaging (e.g.,
lead from lead-lined cans), pesticides or other toxins
sprayed on crops, or mercury found in some fish—all of
which are considered to be food contaminants and which
are discussed in chapters 2 and 12.

Genetic Modification. In the 1970s, scientists found
ways to isolate specific genes (minute segments of DNA,
the molecules that determine traits such as color, size,
and texture) and insert them into other organisms. At
first, this new technology was used to develop medical
products, such as genetically engineered human insulin
for people who have diabetes. By the early 1990s, however, researchers had found ways to take genes from
plants, animals, and even bacteria, and insert them into
plants, say, a tomato, thus creating a new, genetically
modified version of tomato.

Some experts say genetic engineering of foods will provide tremendous benefits to humankind, because it will
allow the production of healthier crops, have less impact
on the environment, and result in greater crop yields.
Others point out that scientists know little or nothing
about how the new organisms they create will affect peo-

ple's health (e.g., causing allergic reactions or triggering unexpected chemical reactions) or how they will interact with other plants, animals, and insects in the environment. Thus the topic of genetically modified foods is a controversial one, and one we explore in depth in chapter 5.

Irradiation. Irradiation of food is a process in which X-rays, electron beams, and gamma rays are used to "zap" certain foods in an attempt to destroy harmful elements, such as disease-causing bacteria. (For the record, the FDA considers irradiation to be a food additive, but for our purposes, we discuss it separately.) Irradiation is not foolproof, however, because it does not destroy viruses or prions (highly infectious substances that can damage the brain and nervous system; they are associated with mad cow disease, see chapter 10) and is not a substitute for adequate storage, preparation, and cooking of foods, all of which can have an effect on food safety. Therefore irradiated beef, if not cooked thoroughly, can still cause food poisoning.

Much of the controversy surrounding the irradiation of food has centered around the treatment of meat and poultry. (As of 2003, only about 5 percent of meat and poultry in the United States was being irradiated.) Meat and poultry are not the only foods that are being treated, however. In fact, the first FDA-approved use of irradiation was for wheat and wheat flour in 1963. Spices, herbs, and vegetable flavorings have been approved for irradiation since 1985, and eggs since 2000. The pros and cons of using irradiation to treat these and other foods are explored in depth in chapter 6.

Other Food Preservation Methods. In addition to using some chemical additives that are preservatives (included under the "Food Additives" heading), food manufacturers also use other methods not only to preserve foods, but also to help eliminate potentially harmful organisms that can cause foodborne illness. These other approaches include:

- Drying: Prevents rotting of meat, the germination of stored grains, and sprouting of certain vegetables, such as potatoes and onions.
- Heating: Can increase shelf life temporarily by sterilizing food. The development of heat sterilization as the basis of what is now the canning industry resulted from Napoleon's offer of a reward for anyone who could find a way to preserve food for his army. Thank goodness—where would we be without canned food?
- Freezing: Originated among ancient peoples living in cold climates, who discovered that they could preserve foods indefinitely.
- Fermentation: Use of enzymes to promote gradual chemical change. Pickling is a very early form of preservation; fermented beverages (e.g., wine, beer) also have a long history, with evidence of fermented beverages found in ancient Egypt and Mesopotamia.

Unintentional Manipulation

In this category are substances that get into our food supply unintentionally. Examples include bacteria and other disease-causing microorganisms (e.g., E. coli, salmonella), mercury (found in fish) and other heavy metals like lead and cadmium; polychlorinated biphenyls (PCBs—industrial chemicals); and volatile organic compounds (types of industrial chemicals). Of these substances, the ones that are most common and that cause the most health problems are microorganisms, which are responsible for millions of cases of food poisoning and thousands of deaths from this diarrheal illness each year. (Read about PCBs and volatile organic compounds in chapter 4; mercury in chapter 12.)

FOOD POISONING

Food poisoning, also known as foodborne disease, is caused by microorganisms—bacteria, parasites, and viruses—that get into the food and/or water supply. The result is often symptoms such as nausea, vomiting, stomach cramps, and diarrhea that can range from mild to severe or even deadly, especially for people who are highly vulnerable, such as the very young, the elderly, pregnant women, and people who have a compromised immune system or chronic illness. These microorganisms are usually transmitted by what is called the fecal-oral route, which means that microorganisms found in animal or human waste get into the food or water we consume. (See Table 1 for a list of organisms commonly associated with food poisoning.)

Microorganisms can contaminate food anywhere along the food production and preparation process: they can be in the soil in the fields, in the feed given to chickens and other livestock, among carcasses in slaughterhouses, in the water used to wash produce at the packing plant, or transmitted from raw meat to vegetables on a cutting board in your kitchen. Thus any type of food—meats, poultry, cheese, milk, fish, fruits and vegetables, and grains—can become contaminated with microorganisms. Although food producers take precautions every step of the way, it's still critically important for you as a consumer to properly choose, store, and prepare every food item you buy. Don't worry; we offer you many tips on how to do just that throughout this book, and especially in chapters 7 through 13.

No one knows exactly how many millions of Americans get food poisoning each year. Because several government agencies are involved in making sure the food supply is safe, there are political and economic reasons why these agencies don't want the number to be too high. The Centers for Disease Control and Prevention (CDC) estimates that 76 million Americans per year get food poisoning, 325,000 need hospitalization, and more

Table 1
Organisms Associated with Food Poisoning

ORGANISM	FOUND IN	ONSET/SYMPTOMS
Bacillus cereus	F&V, grains, spices	6-15 hrs; cramps, abdominal pain, watery diarrhea
Campylobacter jejuni	Meat, poultry, dairy	12-36 hrs; cramps, vomiting, diarrhea, fever, headache
Clostridium botulinum	F&V, fish, seafood, grains	4-24 hrs; muscle paralysis in throat, neck, chest, and extremities, death
Escherichia coli	Meat, poultry, fish, seafood, dairy, F&V, spices	6-24 hrs; there are several strains of E. coli, but symptoms are similar and include diarrhea (may be bloody), abdominal cramps, dehydration, kidney failure
Listeria monocytogenes	Meat, poultry, dairy	24+ hrs; meningitis, encephalitis, death
Salmonella species	Meat, poultry, fish, seafood, dairy, eggs, grains, spices, oil-based foods	8-24 hrs; diarrhea, dehydration, fever, vomiting, abdominal cramps, headache
Shigella species	Fish, seafood, grains	12-36+ hrs; severe bloody diarrhea, abdominal cramps, dehydration
Staphylococcus aureus	Meat, poultry, fish, seafood, dairy, F&V, grains, oil-based foods	½-6 hrs; severe nausea, vomiting, diarrhea, cramps
Streptococcus species	Dairy	24-73 hrs; painful swallowing, sore throat, fever, headache, tonsillitis
Yersinia enterocolitica	Meat, poultry, dairy	6-24 hrs; severe abdominal pain, headache, nausea, diarrhea
Ascaris lumbricoides, Trichinella spiralis (Roundworms)	Contaminated raw meat or vegetables (Ascaris); contaminated meat, mainly pork and wild game (Trichinella)	Long-term: abdominal pain, nausea, vomiting (Ascaris); fever, severely painful inflamed muscles (Trichinella)
Toxoplasma gondii	Undercooked meat	Long-term: affects nerve and muscle tissue; can be deadly for infants
Taenia saginata	Undercooked beef	Long-term: abdominal pain, nervousness, weight loss
Hepatitis A	Wide range of foods	24-72 hrs; abdominal pain, muscle pain, fever, weakness, loss of appetite, digestive distress

than 5,000 die. Yet many scientists say their calculations place the number of cases closer to 80 million per year, with 9,000 or more deaths.

The main reason why it's hard to know exactly how many cases of food poisoning occur in the United States each year is that most people treat themselves. Symptoms of food poisoning are often passed off as "stomach flu," and many people don't bother to go to a doctor and get a culture to identify why they felt sick. Experts in foodborne illnesses believe that for every case of food poisoning that is reported by a doctor, as many as several hundred others are not.

One of the goals of this book is to help you take the right steps to avoid ever being one of these cases. In Part II, we offer you tips on how to avoid food poisoning and describe how you can report suspected cases and learn about food recalls—especially for meat, poultry, and dairy products—to protect your family against potentially deadly illness.

BOTTOM LINE

In today's complex society, we have handed over control of our food supply to a wide range of companies, agencies, and individuals, all of whom have the potential to improve, maintain, or detract from the quality of the food we eat. Although this chapter has only scratched the surface of the huge food production machine in the United States, it gives you a glimpse of what you need to look for when buying and preparing food for your family.

In the next chapter we expand that glimpse and take a closer look at one segment of the food production process, conventionally produced food.

CHAPTER 2

Conventionally Produced Food

The majority of food in the United States—95 percent or more of the fruits, vegetables, grains, meats, eggs, and dairy products—is produced conventionally. For our purposes, in this chapter "conventionally produced food" includes those that have been intentionally exposed to pesticides. Thus this chapter is concerned with the use of chemicals on food crops, such as fruits, vegetables, grains, seeds, and nuts. Conventionally produced food also typically includes items that contain certain additives (including hormones and antibiotics given to livestock and fish), have undergone irradiation, or are the result of genetic manipulation. These latter three topics are discussed in separate, subsequent chapters.

Although Americans are buying more organic foods than they ever did before, most people in the United States fill their shopping carts with foods that likely have been exposed to pesticides, hormones, steroids, or antibiotics. Because conventionally grown produce and grains as well as conventionally raised animal products make up the majority of the American diet, you need to understand the advantages and disadvantages of this way of providing food for your family and what they mean to your health and well-being, as well as to the planet and future generations.

WHAT ARE PESTICIDES?

Pesticides are synthetically produced substances that are used to protect plants and plant products from pests, such as bacteria, insects, mold, rodents, and weeds. In the United States, farmers apply approximately 800 million to 1 billion pounds of pesticides to their crops each year.

Pesticides are available as:

- antimicrobials, which control bacteria.
- fungicides, which control fungus and mold.
- herbicides, which control weeds.
- insecticides, which control insects. There are more than 600 insecticides registered with the Environmental Protection Agency (EPA).
- rodenticides, which control rodents.

Who Monitors Pesticide Use?

Monitoring food safety and pesticide use is a joint effort, as well as a complicated one. The EPA sets the limits (called "tolerances") on how much pesticide residue is allowed to remain on your food. The agency also regulates which pesticides and how much of each one farmers are authorized to use for individual crops. This doesn't mean that farmers will use all 88 pesticides that are allowed to be used on lentils, for example, but it does give them many options from which to choose.

The Food and Drug Administration (FDA) and the US Department of Agriculture (USDA) also team up to monitor our food supply. One of their tasks is to track food that crosses state lines to ensure pesticide limits are not exceeded. Another is a program called the Total Diet Study, in which samples of more than 280 different foods are analyzed for pesticide content, as well as other undesirable substances. We discuss the Total Diet Study in detail and how you can use its results to help you make informed food choices in Part II.

Better Protection for Children

To help toughen the tolerances established by the EPA, President Bill Clinton signed into law the Food Quality Protection Act of 1996, which tightened the standards already in place for pesticide use on food. Essentially, the new law required that the EPA consider the health of infants and children when it determined the acceptable levels of pesticide residues in the US food supply, and it set pesticide residue standards that are ten times stricter than those said to be safe for adults.

This is a significant step. Children are much more susceptible to harm from pesticides in food than are adults because, pound for pound of body weight, they consume more foods that can have high levels of pesticides. Health problems caused in children by pesticides include damage to the nervous system, cancer, and damage to the reproductive system. (Read more about pesticides and children in chapter 3.)

The new law also meant that the EPA had to reassess all existing pesticide tolerances over a ten-year period and meet interim deadlines every three years. In addition, the EPA had to review and assess the worst, most dangerous tolerances first. Unfortunately, the agency failed to meet its deadlines, partly because of pressure from industry and political circles to keep pesticides on the market.

ARGUMENT: WE NEED PESTICIDES

Before World War II, most farmers grew several different crops on their land and rotated them every season or every year. This system of crop rotation makes it difficult for certain insects, like cucumber beetles, corn borers, potato bugs, and squash bugs, to take control of a given crop. Thus farmers had little or no use for pesticides; rotation of crops, along with tilling in animal manure, helped renourish the soil.

Since World War II, however, the trend has been to

form large commercial farms, which focus on one crop only, a system called monoculture. This system created a virtual picnic for pests. Therefore, to help prevent their crops from being ruined by an increasing number of damaging insects and plant diseases, farmers turned to pesticides.

For better or for worse, many of the chemicals developed during World War II were given a new life after that war ended to fight a new war against crop pests. Proponents of pesticide use on food crops argue that these synthetic chemicals are, at least for now, the best weapons we have to help ensure an adequate food supply. According to the American Farm Bureau Federation, pesticides:

- Reduce the risks of crop failure due to insects, rodents, microorganisms, fungi, and weeds.
- Allow greater yields per acre, which keeps other land free for wildlife and other uses.
- Help keep farmers' costs, and thus the price to consumers, down.
- Allow more food to be grown in the United States and reduce our need to import it.

Another argument by some advocates of pesticide use is that these chemicals don't really cause a major health risk. One bit of research that backs this claim is from the National Research Council, which stated in a 1996 report that "the synthetic chemicals in our diet are far less numerous than the natural and have been more thoroughly studied, monitored, and regulated. Their potential biologic effect is lower."

Many other reports, however, point to various health problems associated with pesticide use, especially for children, which are discussed in chapter 3. These health concerns, along with increasing demand for pesticide-free foods and rising production costs for conventional farming, are causing some farmers to reduce their use of synthetic chemicals.

REDUCING PESTICIDE EXPOSURE

How Farmers Can Reduce Pesticide Use

More and more farmers are reevaluating how they use pesticides and are finding ways to reduce the amounts or types they apply to their crops. Rather than routinely spraying entire fields with pesticides, some farmers monitor their crops to see if pest problems are really so bad and only spray when absolutely necessary. Others are slowly adopting methods used by organic farmers, such as introducing beneficial insects to control damaging pests or building up the soil using natural substances (see chapter 3 for more on organic farming methods). Still others are planting their crops closer together, which helps prevent weeds from growing and thus reduces the need for herbicides.

How You Can Reduce Pesticide Exposure

As a consumer, you have some control over the amount of pesticides to which you expose yourself and your family on the foods you eat. Basically, you can either avoid them as much as possible by buying organic foods, or you can reduce your exposure by choosing certain foods over others and by preparing those you do choose in specific ways. We discuss these options in detail in Part II of this book.

FOOD CROP PESTICIDES: A BRIEF LOOK

Farmers in the United States have more than 400 pesticides from which to choose when treating their crops. Each of these substances contains both active ingredients, which are designed to kill specific pests, and inert ingredients, which do not have a direct role in destroying pests.

In addition, pesticides break down into substances called metabolites, which can be more toxic than the original, or "parent," pesticide. For example, malathion, an organophosphate that is widely used on food crops, has a metabolite that is more toxic than malathion itself.

Thus, in addition to the more than 400 pesticides on the market, there are hundreds of metabolites to consider when looking at how food crops may be contaminated.

More than 50 of the pesticides used in agriculture have been classified by the EPA to be possible or probable human carcinogens. Many of these pesticides, such as alachlor and lindane, continue to be used on food crops in the United States, yet the EPA claims that human exposure to these pesticides is within safe limits. Many experts and other individuals don't believe this is true, especially because many of the studies from which they arrived at these conclusions were done on laboratory animals, and no one knows how transferable the results are from animals to humans.

Another reason for doubt is that people don't consume just one pesticide a day, but dozens of them at every meal. No one knows the cumulative effect these pesticides can have on human health. So far, there is evidence—and in some cases strong evidence—that many pesticides are linked to or can cause cancer, birth defects, miscarriages, sterility, immune system disorders, nerve damage, brain dysfunction, and impaired fertility. What we do know is that 25 percent of people in the United States today will develop cancer during their lifetime. Exactly how much of the cancer is caused by pesticide exposure is not known. (In fact, experts estimate that everyone on Earth today has at least 700 contaminants in his or her body, and we know little about the health impact of many of them.) However, the significant increase in the use of pesticides in agriculture (as well as home and general use, such as on golf courses, public parks, and school grounds) during the past few decades has been accompanied by a parallel increase in the incidence of diseases like cancer that have been linked with environmental toxins.

PESTICIDES: WHAT FARMERS ARE USING

Hundreds of pests and organisms can threaten to destroy food crops, so many farmers turn to pesticides. Not all pesticides are created equal, and farmers have several categories from which to choose for their needs. Let's look at four major categories used by US farmers that affect our food supply.

Organophosphates (OPs)

Organophosphates are a class of pesticides, mostly insecticides, that are derived from phosphoric acid. They are the most widely used insecticides; not only are they used on food crops, but they are also applied in homes and family gardens, and used by veterinarians. Organophosphates do not linger in the environment, but because they are used so widely and can be found on so many food products, concern about exposure to them is related to their chronic presence and possible cumulative effects.

Farmers like organophosphates because they are relatively inexpensive and because they are generally more effective than other types of insecticides. Organophosphates kill insects by damaging an enzyme in their body, which then disrupts their nervous system. So far, insects have not developed resistance to organophosphates as they have to some other pesticides. Currently there are about 40 different types of organophosphates from which farmers can choose. The ten most commonly used are listed on p. 24. You'll be seeing these names again and again when we look at pesticide residues in foods in Part II of this book.

The two most common ways people are exposed to organophosphates are in fields that have been treated with the pesticides (e.g., farm workers, or children who play in treated areas) or through contaminated food and water. People who are exposed to significant levels of organophosphates through any of these routes may suffer damage to their nervous system and experience headache, nausea, vomiting, dizziness, weakness, salivation, watery eyes, and diarrhea.

According to the EPA, approximately 60 million pounds of organophosphates are applied to about 60 million acres of agricultural crops in the United States each

---

Most Commonly Used Organophosphates in the United States

(EPA Estimates)

1. Malathion
2. Chlorpyrifos
3. Terbufos
4. Diazinon
5. Methyl parathion
6. Phorate
7. Acephate
8. Azinphosmethyl
9. Phosmet
10. Dimethoate

---

year. How does that break down? Nearly one-third (19 million pounds) is applied to corn, 9 million pounds are reserved for fruits and nuts, and 7 million pounds are applied to vegetables. Much of the remaining organophosphates are applied to cotton.

Organochlorines

Perhaps the most commonly recognized names in this category of pesticides are DDT (dichlorodiphenyltrichloroethane), which was originally used during World War II to kill lice among soldiers, prisoners, and refugees, and to kill other insects that caused malaria and typhus; and Agent Orange, sprayed extensively during the Vietnam War. After World War II, DDT became a popular pesticide for agricultural crops, and it was soon joined by other organochlorines, including aldrin, dieldrin, and toxaphene.

Then in 1962, marine biologist Rachel Carson exposed the dangers of DDT and other chemicals like it in her book *Silent Spring*, where she explained how these substances were contaminating the environment and endangering human, animal, and plant life. In 1972, the EPA banned DDT, and other organochlorines (aldrin, dieldrin, arochlor, chlordane, heptachlor, mirex, hexachlorobenzene, oxychlordane, and toxaphene, among others) were soon banned as well. And for good reason: Organochlorines have been linked with cancer, neurological damage, Parkinson's disease, respiratory illness, abnormal immune system function, and birth defects, and may disrupt hormone function (e.g., the thyroid and sex hormones). Recent studies show that very low exposure in the womb can cause irreversible damage to the immune and reproductive systems of a fetus.

Even though these organochlorines have been banned for many years, traces of them still linger in the environment and get into our food and water supplies. Thus, for example, when you read chapter 12 on dairy products, you will see that the FDA continues to find traces of dieldrin in milk, and in chapter 10 on meat, that hexachlorobenzene is still found in lamb chops.

A few organochlorines still remain on the market and are used on various food crops. Endosulfan, for example, is applied to more than 60 vegetables, fruits, nuts, and cereal grains. In a November 2003 study, researchers found evidence that this organochlorine damages the reproductive system and hormones in young males. The study, which was conducted in India, was the first one that looked at the effects of endosulfan in humans.

Among other organochlorines still on the market are lindane, which is used on grains; dicofol, on apples, citrus, strawberries, beans, peppers, tomatoes, pecans, and walnuts; and methoxychlor, on vegetables and grains.

Carbamates

Like organophosphates, carbamates kill pests by disrupting the nervous system. Unfortunately, at high levels they can have the same effect on humans and result in symptoms like those caused by organophosphates. Carbaryl is the most widely used carbamate insecticide; carbofuran, methomyl, oxaml, and thiodicarb are also on the market. Some of the crops treated with carbamates include, but are not limited to, apples, asparagus, beans, blueberries, broccoli, brussels sprouts, cabbage, cauliflower, corn, cranberries, eggplant, endive, lettuce, mustard greens, peaches, peas, peppers, potatoes, and spinach. Some carbamates can cause cancer and/or may disrupt hormone function.

Pyrethroid Pesticides

These pesticides were developed as a synthetic version of the naturally occurring pesticide called pyrethrin, which is found in chrysanthemums. Some of the pyrethroids used on food crops include cyfluthrin, cypermethrin, esfenvalerate, fenpropathrin, and permethrin. Although the EPA says pyrethroids are not generally considered to be cancer-causing agents, permethrin is a weak carcinogen and cypermethrin has been identified by the EPA as a possible carcinogen. Pyrethroid pesticides are often applied to apples, beans, broccoli, brussels sprouts, cabbage, cauliflower, corn, cucumbers, eggplant, lettuce, mustard greens, peaches, peas, peppers, potatoes, soybeans, spinach, and tomatoes.

BOTTOM LINE

The majority of food available in the United States has been produced using conventional methods, which means it has been exposed to pesticides, antibiotics, hormones, and/or additives, as well as irradiation or genetic modification. As a concerned consumer, you should make yourself aware of the benefits and risks of each of these ways your food can be manipulated, and then take whatever steps you believe are best for you and your family, whether it be purchasing organic foods whenever possible, reducing or eliminating your consumption of some foods and replacing them with healthier choices, or being more vigilant about how you clean, store, and prepare certain foods. Suggestions on how to accomplish all of these options are covered in Part II of this book.

CHAPTER 3

Organically Produced Foods

You're standing in the produce aisle in the supermarket, staring at the tomatoes. In one compartment there are conventionally grown tomatoes; in another, organically grown tomatoes. Which ones should you choose? Are organic tomatoes a healthier choice than conventionally grown ones?

You can't make up your mind, so you wander over to the meat counter, where you see two signs: organically raised beef and regular beef. What's the difference? How do you know which one is better for your family, and why?

You're still unsure about what to buy, so you walk over to the dairy case, where you see organic milk next to the regular milk, and organic cheeses next to the conventional ones. You're beginning to think, "Gee, it was much easier to shop when I didn't have to make so many decisions about what to buy." But you've heard that organic foods are better for you, and you do want the best for your family. With the increasing number and variety of organic products on the market, you are wondering, "What do I really know about organic foods?"

Many people are asking that question. And as they do, the sale of organic foods has been rising: It generates about $10 billion per year and is the fastest growing segment of the food industry. In this chapter we answer your questions about organically produced foods, including what "organic" means, the health benefits you and your family can derive from eating organic foods, and what some of the downsides may be.

WHAT DOES "ORGANIC" MEAN?

According to the United States Department of Agriculture (USDA), which oversees the National Organic Program that was instituted in October 2002, "Organic food is produced by farmers who emphasize the use of renewable resources and the conservation of soil and water to enhance environmental quality for future generations. Organic meat, poultry, eggs, and dairy products come from animals that are given no antibiotics or growth hormones. Organic food is produced without using most conventional pesticides, petroleum-based fertilizers or sewage sludge–based fertilizers, bioengineering [genetically modified], or ionizing radiation."

Respect for Soil and Water

Now let's translate that statement for you. When it comes to conservation of soil and water, organic farmers take special care. They realize that soil is a living organism that must be nurtured and protected if it's going to continue to produce healthy crops, and that water is a precious resource. So they use techniques such as the following:

- Cover crops: Crops such as bell beans, vetch (a type of legume), and Austrian field peas are planted during the off-season, allowed to grow, then plowed under while they are still young, as they provide an excellent source of fertilizer (as nitrogen) and discourage disease-causing bacteria in the soil.
- Compost: This rich natural fertilizer is the result of the decomposition of plant products by earthworms and microorganisms. National standards require that organic farmers wait until their compost reaches a

temperature of 131 degrees for at least three days
before they till it into the soil. That's the temperature at which harmful organisms become harmless.
- Drip irrigation: This allows water to be delivered
  directly to the crops, which reduces water waste and
  also helps control growth of weeds.

Saying No to Antibiotics and Hormones

Farmers who produce organic meats, poultry, eggs, and
dairy products do not give their animals feed that contains
antibiotics or growth hormones. It's estimated that up to
70 percent of the antibiotics produced in the United States
are fed to livestock raised for human consumption, and
while some of these antibiotics are used to treat diseased
animals, most of them are used solely for profit: They make
animals fatter, faster. When antibiotics are used in this way,
they greatly increase the chance that bacteria resistant to
these drugs will develop. In fact, bacterial resistance to antibiotics is a serious problem in the United States. Antibiotic-
resistant bacteria on food can cause food poisoning that is
difficult to treat.

The use of growth hormones received a lot of press
beginning in 1994, when some dairy farmers started to
give their cows a bovine growth hormone (BGH) called
Posilac. Use of BGH causes cows to increase their milk
production by about 10 percent, resulting in more product (and profits) for farmers. At the same time, BGH
increases the risk of infections and other health problems
in treated cows, and some experts report that the hormone is risky for humans as well. (Since BGH is a food
additive, we discuss it in more detail in chapter 4.)

Saying No to Pesticides

Finally, the wording of the USDA statement is "most
conventional pesticides," which means some are still allowed under this program. The allowable pesticides include bacterial sprays and sulfur, which some experts say

are safe. To ensure that organically grown crops are not contaminated by pesticides that drift over from neighboring farms that use poisons, the USDA has set standards for how far away two such farms must be from each other. This does not guarantee that a minute amount of pesticides might not make their way into organic territory, but the risk is greatly minimized.

One question people often ask is, if organic farmers don't use pesticides, how do they control pests and diseases on their crops? The answer is, they use a variety of natural, holistic approaches, including:

- Beneficial insects: Use of ladybugs, lacewings, certain wasps, and other insects, which feast on crop-destroying bugs, such as aphids (favorite food of ladybugs), caterpillars, and beetles.
- Trap crops: Crops that are usually planted around the borders of fields and act as a mating area and haven for beneficial insects. Trap crops might be thought of as dormitories for the working beneficial insects.
- Crop rotation: The habit of changing the crops, each season, that grow in a particular area of the farm. This helps prevent pest populations and diseases from becoming entrenched in a given area. Thus, a farmer might grow lettuce in area A and broccoli in area B one season, then switch to spinach and carrots, respectively, the next season.
- Utilize and attract wildlife: Animals, such as frogs, toads, snakes, birds, turtles, and spiders, that feast on pest insects. One toad, for example, can eat about 3,000 insects per month. Organic farmers often attract insect-eating birds like purple martins by setting out birdhouses near their fields.

Although the word "natural" doesn't appear in the USDA statement, the first thing many people think of when they hear "organic" is "natural." However, "natural" and "organic" are *not* the same thing. Many things are "natural," but they are far from organic. Manure is natural, but it's not necessarily organic.

Labeling Organic Foods

Organic foods are now easier to recognize in the supermarket, although the meaning behind their labels is not clear. Foods that sport a 100 PERCENT ORGANIC label must contain organic ingredients only. A label that merely says ORGANIC means that at least 95 percent of the ingredients in the product, by fluid volume or weight (not including salt and water), must be organic. If a product is labeled MADE WITH ORGANIC INGREDIENTS, it means that at least 70 percent of the ingredients must be organic. Read labels carefully before making your purchases.

BENEFITS OF ORGANIC FARMING

Reduced Exposure to Pesticides

This is the number one reason people choose to buy and eat organically produced foods. But notice we say "reduced exposure to pesticides" and not "complete elimination of pesticides." Although organic food is not produced or treated with pesticides or chemicals, these poisons are ubiquitous in our environment and sometimes are carried by air, water, or soil from nearby pesticide-treated crops or other sources. Two recent examples illustrate this situation.

In 2003, there was contamination of lettuce and other vegetables grown in California, Arizona, and Nevada that were irrigated with water from the Colorado River, water that had been contaminated with perchlorate, a substance found in rocket fuel. Lockheed Martin, the giant aerospace and defense contractor, was dumping perchlorate into the river, and reportedly had known since 1997 that vegetables can store high concentrations of the chemical, but it had not reported this fact to the EPA or health authorities. All of this information was made public by the Environmental Working Group from test documents that it obtained. Perchlorate impairs function of the thyroid, damaging its ability to produce hormones and take in iodide. The documents showed that the vegetables tested had an average of more than 2,600 micrograms of perchlorate per kilogram, which is thousands of times greater than what the EPA considers to be safe.

In 2002, a study conducted by the Consumers Union found that 75 percent of conventionally produced food contained pesticide residue, compared with 23 percent of organically produced foods. Does this mean you should shun organic produce? Experts agree that the nutritional benefits you derive from fruits and vegetables far outweigh the risks of exposure to pesticides. Edward Groth, a senior scientist for Consumers Union, notes, "Less is better. Fewer residues and lower levels of residues are better than higher levels of residues and more residues."

Health Risks From Pesticides. If you were to take an overdose of, say, aspirin, you would experience ill effects immediately, such as nausea, vomiting, delirium tremens, ringing in your ears, dizziness, or loss of consciousness. Yet when you ingest minute amounts of pesticides and toxic chemicals, they typically accumulate slowly in the body, over time, as you consume them day after day. Research shows that the potential health problems from these poisons can take years to appear. This delayed reaction makes it easy for people to forget that what they eat today can harm them tomorrow.

One of the most important things to remember about pesticides and other contaminants in our food is this: We are exposed to not just one herbicide or insecticide or fungicide, but to a mixture of these toxins in our food every day of our lives. The effects on the body of several pesticides may be hundreds of times more potent than the effects of just one pesticide by itself. The EPA has considered the impact of only single pesticides on health when it set tolerance levels.

We certainly can't intentionally expose people to pesticides to see how they affect their health, which would be a clear way to link pesticide exposure and illness. Many experts believe, however, that the residues of some pesticides increase the risk of cancer, damage the nervous system and endocrine system, cause allergic reactions, and contribute to multiple chemical sensitivity.

Yet there have been some isolated, acute cases that show how damaging pesticides can be. In 1985, about a thousand people in Canada and several western US states became very ill after they ate watermelons that had been treated illegally with the insecticide aldicarb. Even though the level of pesticide on the watermelons was estimated to be well below a level that would cause illness, the individuals experienced nausea, vomiting, muscle weakness, seizures, abnormal heartbeat, and blurry vision within a few hours of eating the fruit.

Other evidence of the dangers of pesticide use can be found among children who live in agricultural communities or those of migrant workers. Among children in McFarland, California, for example, the cancer rate is three times the national average. Experts believe this is related to the fact that the area uses more pesticides than most other counties in the state. In major agricultural areas in Minnesota, babies born to fathers who work as pesticide applicators have more birth defects than other infants.

Pesticides and Your Children's Health. "I've heard that fruits and vegetables are treated with lots of pesticides, so is it safe for my two-year-old to eat grapes and carrots and other produce?" Experts agree that even though pesticides are often found on conventionally grown produce (the highest levels of insecticides and fungicides are applied to fruits and vegetables), fruits and vegetables provide many more health advantages than detriments. Naturally, you want to limit your child's—and your own—exposure to pesticides as much as possible, and we tell you how you can do that in chapter 7.

But the concern voiced by this parent is valid. Children consume higher concentrations of pesticides because of their diet and their smaller body size. Pound for pound of body weight, for example, the typical one-year-old eats two to seven times more broccoli, carrots, grapes, and pears, all of which can have high levels of pesticides, than older children and adults. They also consume more winter squash and peaches, both of which have very high levels of pesticide residues, according to research conducted by the Consumers Union in 1999.

Just how significant those pesticide levels can be was shown in several studies. One, conducted by the University of Washington, looked at thirty-nine preschool children and compared pesticide levels in children who ate organically grown produce compared with those who ate conventionally grown fruits and vegetables. Children who ate organic fruits and vegetables had pesticide concentrations six times lower than children who ate conventionally grown produce. The researchers looked at organophosphates (OPs) in particular, as these insecticides are widely used in the United States, are associated with damage to the nervous system, and are easy to detect in urine samples. (Read more about organophosphates in chapter 2.)

Similar results were found in another study, which looked at ninety-six children. In this study, OP levels were found in the urine of all children except one, and that one child ate only organic produce.

Pesticides and Prenatal Health. If you're pregnant or have ever been pregnant, you know that you need to be concerned about your child's health even before he or she is born. A developing fetus is extremely vulnerable to outside forces, including whatever a mother puts into her body. Hundreds of studies show the dangers of smoking, drinking alcohol, and using drugs during pregnancy, yet experts know very little about the impact of pesticides on a human fetus.

But there are some things scientists do know, and one

is that a fetus, as well as an infant up to age six months, does not have a blood-brain barrier, a system which prevents poisons from getting into the brain. Therefore, pesticides or other contaminants that can affect the neurological system have a clear pathway to the brain. Experts also know that the placenta, which is well-equipped to keep viruses and bacteria out of the womb, is not designed to prevent pesticides from contaminating the fluid that surrounds the fetus.

Several studies point to a link between pesticides and birth defects. In one study in Minnesota, for example, researchers found a higher rate of birth defects among children born to parents who worked as pesticide applicators than among the general population in the region. The investigators also found a link between specific types of pesticides; for example, use of phosphine was associated with a greater risk of central nervous system or neurobehavioral disorders (e.g., autism, attention deficit hyperactivity disorder) than among controls.

Yet another study, this one in Montana, South and North Dakota, and Minnesota, looked at more than 43,000 births from 1995 to 1997 in wheat-producing counties. Dr. Dina Schreinemachers and her colleagues found that rates of respiratory, circulatory, and musculoskeletal birth defects were twice as common in counties that produce a lot of wheat. They also found that males conceived during April or June, when pesticide application is at its peak, were nearly five times as likely to have birth defects compared with males conceived during other times of the year.

Findings like these have caused concerned individuals to form organizations like Mothers of Organics, which urges pregnant women to be especially mindful of the foods they eat. They are not eating just for themselves but for the future health of their child. Ways to avoid and reduce pesticide consumption are discussed in Part II.

More Nutritious

Some people argue that organic foods are much more nutritious than those produced conventionally. A study published in the *Journal of Alternative and Complementary Medicine* compiled the results from thirty-seven other studies of nutrient levels in organic foods and found that organic produce had higher percentages of boron (40% more than seen in conventionally grown foods), calcium (27%), chromium (86%), iron (20%), magnesium (28%), phosphorus (13%), potassium (11%), selenium (372%), and zinc (8%).

Another study, this one at the University of California, Davis, found that organically and sustainably grown strawberries, blackberries, and corn had up to 58 percent more polyphenolics, substances that act as antioxidants and may protect against cancer and heart disease, when compared with the same crops grown conventionally. The organically and sustainably grown crops also had more ascorbic acid, which the body transforms into vitamin C.

Environmentally Friendly

That organically produced crops are more environmentally friendly than conventionally grown produce is a subject of debate. Points in favor of organic farming include the following:

- Organic farming promotes biodiversity, which means the native species and ecology are better preserved. Because organic farmers don't use pesticides or chemical fertilizers, fewer earthworms (critical for good soil health), insects, rodents, and birds are killed. Natural order is maintained.
- Because synthetic pesticides are not used, organic farmers don't pollute the soil, air, or water.
- Organic farmers who raise livestock don't give their animals antibiotics. Antibiotic resistance among people is a serious problem, and many experts agree

that the presence of antibiotics in meat and dairy products is contributing to this problem. Organic farmers do their part to help reduce antibiotic resistance.

- Farmers who raise livestock organically also don't inject their animals with hormones.
- Organic farming methods depend less on fossil fuels and thus are more energy efficient than conventional farming. According to the United Kingdom's Department for Environment, Food and Rural Affairs, organic dairy farms use 74 percent less energy than conventional dairy producers. A *Science* article noted that "for most crops, organic plots are more energy efficient per unit crop."

Taste

This is another subject of debate. Taste tests have been conducted, with some people insisting that organic produce tastes better than conventionally grown; others say there's no difference. Some experts say organic produce tastes better because it is usually much fresher than conventionally grown fruits and vegetables, and fresh-picked produce tastes better, regardless of whether it is organic or conventionally grown. Better taste may also be due to the fact that organic produce is allowed to ripen naturally, while conventionally grown items are usually picked early and allowed to ripen while in transit, and/ or treated with gas to ripen unnaturally.

DISADVANTAGES OF ORGANIC FARMING

From an economic point of view, organic farming has a few disadvantages, although these downsides may change in the future. For now, one disadvantage is that organic farming methods, which are more labor intensive, make it more difficult to produce large yields compared with conventional methods. Another disadvantage is that organic farming requires more land, as farmers need to create their own fertilizer and provide plants for beneficial insects. These two issues contribute to yet another economic disadvantage: that organic foods are usually more expensive. As demand increases, however, and new organic farming methods are implemented, costs should come down.

Some people say that organic fruits and vegetables don't always "look as nice" as conventionally grown produce. Sometimes they have blemishes, or they lack the shine that would come from wax applied to their skins, or their color isn't striking because their skins haven't been artificially colored. But years ago, when most people picked their own fruits and vegetables from their farms and backyard gardens, blemishes were expected, and no one would have dreamt of waxing or coloring their food.

BOTTOM LINE

Organically produced foods offer some clear advantages over conventionally produced items, especially when you consider pesticide exposure. Once delegated to specialty stores and hard-to-find back-road farms, organic produce, meats, and dairy products are now commonplace in some mainstream supermarkets and large chain natural food stores. If your favorite food stores don't carry organic foods or they have a poor selection, talk to the manager about your desire to buy organic. Consumer demand will not only help drive up the number of selections, it will also bring down the prices.

Another place to look for organic produce is through Community Supported Agriculture (CSA), a member-supported, direct marketing approach used by many small farms. Here's how it works: Members of a community pay a weekly, monthly, or seasonal fee to a CSA (one or more small farms, often organic) in exchange for regular supplies of fresh produce. The produce in supermarkets is usually seven or more days old, while fruits and vegetables from a CSA are generally delivered within twenty-four hours of picking. Thus they are more nutritious. In addition, CSAs often offer new or heirloom varieties of produce not available in stores, you know where the produce has come from, and you help support a local business. There are approximately 1,000 CSAs in North America. To find if there is one in your area, explore the Web site: www.nal.usda.gov/afsic/csa or www.csacenter.org.

CHAPTER 4

Food Additives and Contaminants

Pick up any package of processed food in the supermarket and read the ingredient list. Do you see a litany of chemical names that you can't pronounce? Have you ever wondered what's really behind the ambiguous words "artificial flavors," "artificial colors," or "preservatives"?

In today's world of mass-produced, factory-made foods, putting chemical additives into our food has become as American as apple pie. But today's apple pie from the supermarket's frozen food department or bakery has a few ingredients not found in the pies your grandmother used to make, ingredients with long, unappetizing chemical names and, in some cases, accompanied by health risks, for you and your children.

Adding these ingredients may not profit you but it does profit someone: According to a study from the Business Communications Company, Inc., the food additives market was nearly $5 billion in 2001, and it is expected to reach $5.8 billion in 2006. It's easy to understand why individuals invested in this industry would not want to see their products declared unsafe or banned, yet there are some people who believe certain additives should meet this fate.

In this chapter we look at some of the most common food additives you can find in your food. We'll tell you which ones are safe, which ones have been poorly tested, and which ones are possibly dangerous. The good news is, most additives appear to be safe, and a few even improve food's nutritional value.

Some other substances can find their way into the food supply uninvited, substances such as industrial chemicals, heavy metals, antibiotics, and hormones. They, too, can have an impact on health, so we talk about what these unwelcome substances are, where they come from, and how you can avoid them.

WHAT ARE FOOD ADDITIVES?

The National Institutes of Health (NIH) defines a food additive as "a substance that becomes part of a food product when it is added (intentionally or unintentionally) during the processing or production of that specific food item." Thus the vitamin D added to milk, as well as the hormones that are fed to the cows that produce milk, are both additives: The vitamin D is intentional, while the hormones are unintentional, because they are not added directly to the milk but are found in small amounts in the milk taken from the cow.

Food additives serve five basic purposes:

- Improve or preserve nutritional value: Foods are often "enriched" or "fortified" with vitamins and/or minerals to make them more nutritious. The irony is that the act of processing foods often strips away the same vitamins and minerals that food manufacturers add back in. Products that have had nutrients added to them must be labeled with this information.
- Help maintain product consistency: In this category are substances such as anticaking additives, emulsifiers, stabilizers, and thickeners.
- Maintain palatability and wholesomeness: Preservatives are added to foods to reduce spoilage that can be caused by bacteria, yeast, air, and fungi; to help baked goods preserve their flavor by preventing oils

and fats from becoming rancid; and to prevent fresh fruits from turning brown.

- Control alkalinity and acidity, and provide leavening: Some additives modify the acidity or alkalinity of foods in an effort to maintain a desirable color and flavor. Leavening agents are added to baked goods to help them rise.
- Enhance flavor and improve color: Colors are added to many foods to improve their appearance, while natural and artificial flavors are added to enhance flavor.

For a complete list, see the box "Types of Food Additives and What They Do."

TYPES OF FOOD ADDITIVES AND WHAT THEY DO

- Anticaking agents: keep powdered products such as flour and salt flowing freely when poured
- Artificial sweeteners: provide a sweet taste for fewer calories than sugar; usually used in "diet" foods such as diet beverages, low-calorie cookies and cakes, and low-calorie frozen desserts
- Colorings: add or restore color to food; may be listed on a label as "certified color," "artificial color," or a specific color followed by a number, such as "yellow no. 5"; used in a wide range of foods
- Color retention agents: help enhance or retain the color of food; used in a wide range of foods
- Emulsifiers: help prevent separation of water and oil mixtures
- Flavorings: restore flavor that is lost during processing; help make food more palatable; used in a wide range of foods
- Flavor enhancers: improve the flavor and/or aroma; used in a wide range of foods

- Flour treatment agents: improve appearance and baking quality
- Food acids: help maintain a steady level of sourness in food
- Glazing agents: provide a protective coating on food; also make foods shiny
- Humectants: prevent foods (e.g., dried fruits) from drying out
- Mineral salts: help improve food texture; often used in processed meats
- Preservatives: help protect against deterioration of food caused by bacteria and other microorganisms; found in a wide range of foods, from baked goods to cereals, canned foods, and frozen foods
- Propellants (gases): help propel food (e.g., spray oils, whipped cream) from a container
- Stabilizers: help maintain a uniform dispersion of ingredients in food
- Thickeners and vegetable gums: improve texture and provide uniform consistency; used in foods like yogurts, cream soups, and gravies

There are more than 3,000 food additives on the FDA's list of "Everything Added to Food in the United States" (EAFUS). You can see the entire list online at http://vm.cfsan.fda.gov/~dms/eafus.html

Who Monitors Food Additive Safety?

The Food and Drug Administration (FDA) regulates the approval, testing, and safety of food additives in the United States under the authority of the Food, Drug and Cosmetic Act of 1938 (with amendments added in 1958 and 1960). Congress has defined safety as "reasonable certainty that no harm will result from use of an additive." This doesn't mean that the FDA doesn't approve substances that can be harmful to animals or humans, however. In fact, the FDA has and continues to approve additives that may cause side effects, but only at a level that is one one-hundredth of the amount considered to be harmful. That means if, say, one teaspoon of substance A is the typical amount someone would consume and research shows that some people may experience side effects if they consume a hundred teaspoons, substance A would be approved.

One of the amendments prohibits the FDA from approving an additive if there is evidence that it causes cancer in animals or humans. However, some studies suggest that a number of approved additives can cause cancer in animals or pose a health risk to certain individuals. A list of some of these additives and a discussion of each can be found later in this chapter under "Additives to Subtract."

How Additives Get Approved

When manufacturers seek approval for a new food additive, specific guidelines are followed:

- The manufacturer must use scientific data to prove to the FDA that the additive does what it was designed to do (e.g., enhance the color of a specific food or prevent it from spoiling) and that it isn't harmful when consumed at a reasonable level.
- The FDA reviews the data and determines whether the additive meets its standards. If it does, the FDA issues standards that regulate the use of the additive. For example, the FDA can control which foods the additive may be used in and the maximum amount that can be added.
- Substances that are being considered as additives in meat and poultry products must be authorized by the US Department of Agriculture along with the FDA.
- Once an additive has been approved, the FDA keeps track of any new research concerning the safety of the substance.
- The FDA also monitors complaints about the addi-

tive from consumers, doctors, and food manufacturers. This system, called the Adverse Reaction Monitoring System (ARMS), helps the FDA determine whether any additive presents a public health risk. (See the Appendix for information on ARMS.)

Not every food additive on the market has undergone this approval process, however. Two categories of food additives—prior-sanctioned additives (approved by the FDA before 1958) and GRAS, Generally Recognized As Safe, which includes those that have been used extensively for decades without causing any known harmful effects—have not. More than 700 additives are contained in these two categories. A few of the items in the prior-sanctioned list include sodium nitrate (which is a known carcinogen; see "Should You Worry about Food Additives?" below), potassium nitrate, calcium phosphate, calcium carbonate, and magnesium stearate. Some of the items on the GRAS list include sugar, salt, vinegar, and guar gum. Here are a few more GRAS additives in their respective categories. If you see any of these ingredients listed on a food item, the government recognizes it as safe:

- **Anticaking agents:** aluminum calcium silicate, calcium silicate, magnesium silicate.
- **Artificial flavors:** acetoin, citral, ethyl vanillin, ethyl ester, vanillin.
- **Chemical preservatives:** ascorbic acid, benzoic acid, gum guaiac, methylparaben, sulfur dioxide.
- **Emulsifiers:** cholic acid, propylene glycol, ox bile extract.
- **Nutrients:** aspartic acid, biotin, calcium oxide, copper gluconate, ferrous lactate, glycine, lysine, potassium chloride, sorbitol, vitamin D2, zinc sulfate.
- **Stabilizers:** acacia, agar-agar, guar gum, sodium alginate.

Should You Worry about Food Additives?

The FDA assures us that the approved food additives are safe and that it is always monitoring and/or evaluating additives to make sure they remain that way. Naturally, nothing is one hundred percent safe for everyone, so there are some precautions to consider.

If, for example, you are allergic to a specific additive, you may experience an allergic reaction to it even though the FDA has determined that the amount allowed in the food item is "safe" for the majority of people. One example is sulfites, an additive that is commonly found in processed meats. Some people have an allergic reaction that can range from a mild rash to life-threatening breathing problems. Therefore, if you or a family member has any allergies or food intolerances, you should always read the labels on any food before you buy it. If you do experience a reaction to a food additive, you are encouraged to contact the FDA's Adverse Reaction Monitoring System so the authorities can monitor whether a specific additive may need to be removed from the market.

Some people are also concerned about other health issues related to food additives, including the risk of cancer. Indeed, some approved food additives have shown evidence of being carcinogenic, and for that reason some people continue to ask the FDA to ban these substances (see "Additives to Subtract").

The following food additives have the approval of the FDA, but not of some experts, consumer groups, and consumers, who worry about the potential for allergic reactions, cancer, birth defects, and other health concerns. Again, it's important to remember that while any one of these or other additives may have tested "safe" when consumed in minute amounts (like the amount found in a normal serving of a food), the fact that you consume dozens of contaminants every day, and that these and other contaminants *accumulate* in the body over time, explains why many experts are concerned about these additives. Here's a brief look at a few of them.

Additives to Subtract

Acesulfame K. This artificial sweetener is 200 times sweeter than sugar and is available under the brand names Sunette and Sweet One. The FDA approved acesulfame K (the "K" is for potassium) in 1988 for use in baked goods, refrigerated and frozen desserts, yogurt, dry dessert mixes, hard and soft candies, table sweeteners, syrup, sweet toppings, and sauces. It has not yet been approved for use in soft drinks.

In laboratory tests, acesulfame K has caused tumors in rats, dogs, and rabbits.

Aspartame. You may know this artificial, no-calorie sweetener better as NutraSweet or Equal. Once you ingest aspartame, it is easily converted into formaldehyde, a known carcinogen. In fact, aspartame causes cancer in animals and has been linked to brain cancer in humans. People who should avoid aspartame include women who are pregnant or lactating, and individuals who have phenylketonuria, a metabolic disorder.

Butylated Hydroxyanisole (BHT). Pick up most boxes of breakfast cereal, turn to the ingredients list, and you're likely to see the words "BHT added to preserve freshness." Butylated hydroxyanisole is a preservative and antioxidant that is found in many commercial foods, especially those children love to eat. Yet how safe is it? In the Tenth Annual Report on Carcinogens (2002), it was stated that BHT was "reasonably anticipated to be a human carcinogen." Its potentially harmful effects were apparently enough to convince the United Kingdom to ban BHT, but it is still legal in the United States. Use of BHT has been associated with liver and kidney damage, behavioral problems, a weakened immune system, birth defects, cancer, and infertility.

Carrageenan. This derivative from red seaweed (*Chondrus crispus*) is a frequent ingredient in puddings, ice cream, cottage cheese, soy milk, rice milk, and toothpaste, among other items, where it is useful as a thickener. Carrageenan is a suspected carcinogen in humans and has been shown to cause intestinal ulcers and irritable bowel disease in animals.

Monosodium Glutamate. This food enhancer, usually abbreviated MSG, is made by fermenting starch with beet sugar, cane sugar, or molasses. It is often associated with food served in Chinese restaurants, when in fact many such restaurants have stopped using this additive. It is, however, still found in a wide variety of processed foods available in supermarkets, often disguised under other names. For example, food labels that list autolyzed yeast, calcium caseinate, gelatin, glutamate, glutamic acid, hydrolyzed protein, sodium caseinate, textured protein, yeast extract, or yeast nutrient always contain MSG. Products that contain disodium guanylate or disodium inosinate are expensive additives that work with MSG, and if either of these additives appears on a label, MSG is probably in the item as well. The Environmental Protection Agency has also approved the use of MSG (in the form of processed free glutamic acid, the toxic ingredient in MSG) as a spray on all crops.

Experts have known about the side effects of MSG since the 1960s, when animal studies showed that it can cause brain lesions and neuroendocrine disorders. Use of MSG in humans has been associated with migraine, seizures, rapid heart beat, rash, and depression. Reactions to MSG can occur immediately or up to forty-eight hours after it is ingested.

Nitrates and Nitrites. Nitrates are naturally occurring chemicals that are created by the breakdown of nitrogen gas, which is found in the body and all around you. Nitrites are created when nitrates break down. Food manufacturers add nitrates and/or nitrites to meats to inhibit the growth of bacterial spores that cause botulism (food poisoning), preserve the flavor of spices in the meat (e.g., sausages, luncheon meats), speed up the curing process, preserve a pleasing color to meat, fish, and poultry, and retard rancidity. Although nitrites are known carcinogens, the FDA approves their use because it has determined that the risk of food poisoning is greater than the risk of cancer from ingesting nitrites. Nitrates themselves are not carcinogens; when nitrates react with amines (which are everywhere, including food, water, and the body), they form nitrosamines, which are cancer-causing substances. Some food manufacturers add antioxidants, such as sodium ascorbate or sodium erythorbate, to foods to which they have added nitrites to inhibit the formation of nitrosamines.

Olestra. Olestra is a no-fat, no-calorie fat replacer that is added to certain high-calorie, high-fat foods, such as potato chips and corn chips, to significantly reduce both fat and calorie content. Olestra also inhibits the absorption of vitamins A, D, E, and K and depletes the body of carotenoids (e.g., beta-carotene, lycopene, and lutein, found in foods such as carrots, tomatoes, and romaine lettuce, respectively). Consuming foods that contain olestra can also lead to abdominal cramping, diarrhea, and fecal urgency. Another reason to be wary of olestra, according to Dr. Walter Willett and Dr. Meir Stampfer, both of the Harvard School of Public Health, is that "there is strong reason to suspect that the effects [of olestra] will include increases in cancer, heart disease, stroke, and blindness."

As of April 2002 the FDA had logged in about 20,000 complaints from consumers about olestra. This is more complaints than the agency has seen for all other additives combined.

Potassium Bromate. This additive is used to strengthen bread dough. In the United States, the Center for Science in the Public Interest (CSPI) has been calling for a ban on potassium bromate for many years, while Canada and the United Kingdom banned its use more than a decade ago. Potassium bromate was first found to cause cancer in lab animals in 1982. In 1991 the FDA urged bakers to stop using potassium bromate but did not ban it, so many still use it. In California, a law was passed requiring bakers in that state who use potassium bromate to label their packages with a warning that the product contains a cancer-causing ingredient. Nationwide, many major baked-good companies have stopped using potassium bromate, although others like Wonder Bread, Home Pride, Sunbeam, and Tastykake still do. Fast-food chains such as Arby's, Burger King, and Wendy's use buns that contain potassium bromate.

Sodium Benzoate. Sodium benzoate is a preservative that causes asthma and rash in sensitive individuals. It can be found in some soft drinks and fruit drinks.

Sulfites. Sulfites are used to prevent discoloration of fruits and vegetables, and in wine-making to inhibit the growth of bacteria. One percent of the general population is sensitive to sulfites, and more than one million people with asthma are sensitive to them as well. The FDA requires manufacturers to list sulfites on food labels when used as a preservative, or even when used only as part of the food processing technique if present at levels of 10 parts per million or higher. Sulfite use on fruits and vegetables in salad bars and grocery stores was banned by the FDA in 1986; however, it is best to ask before eating from a salad bar in an unfamiliar restaurant, as some restaurants still use sulfites.

Sulfur Dioxide. This additive has been known to cause tightness of the chest in people who have asthma. It can also cause rash. Sulfur dioxide can be found in some fruit juices, concentrated soft drink mixes, pickles, dried fruit, beer, and wine.

Tartrazine. Tartrazine, also known as yellow dye no. 5, is a coloring derived from coal tar. The FDA estimates that up to 100,000 Americans are sensitive to tartrazine. They may experience asthmatic symptoms (wheezing, shortness of breath) and rash after ingesting tartrazine. Ironically, tartrazine is used in some medications that are designed to treat asthma. It is also found in many foods, including but not limited to butter, margarine, candy, pudding, ice cream, skim milk, cereals, canned fruit, shrimp, cheese, yogurt, and cake mixes.

Waxed Fruit?

Before you bite into a shiny red apple, do you stop and wonder *why* the apple glows? If it's a conventionally grown apple, it's probably been waxed. Although fruits and vegetables have their own natural wax to protect them, it is removed during processing, when produce is washed repeatedly to remove dirt. Therefore, artificial wax is a food additive that is applied to much of the produce you see in the supermarket, not only to replace the natural wax, but also to:

- Help prevent the growth of mold: Waxes must be combined with chemicals to prevent mold growth.
- Help retain moisture during processing, shipping, and marketing: Most produce is 80 to 95 percent water.
- Prevent bruising and other physical damage
- Improve the appearance of the produce: Waxing will not improve the quality of inferior fruits and vegetables.

Unfortunately, applying synthetic wax also seals in pesticide residues, which means washing the produce won't remove the toxins. You must peel waxed fruits and vegetables if you want to get rid of pesticides that are in the skin. Naturally, peeling produce will not eliminate any pesticides that may have penetrated into the flesh of the fruit or vegetable.

The coating used on produce is called food-grade wax and is derived from plants, petroleum, beeswax, and/or shellac-based wax or resin. All of these coatings must meet EPA regulations and FDA food additive standards and have been shown to be safe to eat. Generally, only a drop or two of wax is used on each piece of produce, and it may be mixed with water or another substance to help it spread evenly over the fruit or vegetable. If you do eat the skins of waxed produce, your body will not digest the wax, which means it will pass through your body without breaking down or being absorbed.

Although you can probably easily identify the waxed fruits and vegetables in the produce aisle, markets are required by federal law to label any produce that has been coated. Signs in the market should say "Coated with food-grade vegetable-, petroleum-, beeswax-, and/or shellac-based wax or resin, to maintain freshness." Produce most likely to be waxed include apples, avocados, bell peppers, cantaloupes, cucumbers, eggplant, grapefruit, lemons, limes, melons, oranges, parsnips, passion fruit, peaches, pineapples, pumpkins, rutabagas, squash, sweet potatoes, tomatoes, turnips, and yucca.

ANTIBIOTICS AND HORMONES

When you get a bacterial infection, your doctor may prescribe an antibiotic. That's how you expect these drugs to be used. But according to the Union of Concerned Scientists, up to 70 percent of antibiotics in the United States are given to farm animals, and not because they're sick. Farmers use antibiotics regularly because they increase the rate at which animals gain weight, which reduces the farmers' cost of producing meat and in turn increases their profit margin.

Similarly, farmers inject hormones (steroids) into beef cattle and sheep to bulk up meat production and into dairy cows to increase milk production. Again, the reason is economics. Unfortunately, these antibiotics and hormones have detrimental effects not only on the animals but also, say many experts, on people as well. Let's look at how antibiotics and hormones can affect us.

Antibiotics

Each year in the United States, 26.6 million pounds of antibiotics are given to food animals, and only 2 million of those pounds are used to treat specific diseases. Another 40,000 to 50,000 pounds of antibiotics are sprayed on fruit trees. While some people argue that there's nothing wrong with giving animals antibiotics in order to increase meat production and improve farmers' profits, scientists have found a link between the use of these antibiotic growth promoters and an increased risk of antibiotic resistance in people. What does that mean to you?

Say, for example, you regularly consume minute amounts of antibiotics in meats and dairy products. If you become ill and your doctor prescribes an antibiotic that normally works against the particular microorganism that is causing the illness, it may *not* work; the disease-causing bacteria may have become resistant to the drug because you have been overexposed to it. Overuse of antibiotics—from taking antibiotics often or indiscriminately for illnesses and/or from chronic exposure in foods you eat, or both—allows only drug-resistant microorganisms to survive, and this situation has mushroomed into a major problem in the United States: antibiotic resistance.

The problem of antibiotic resistance so concerns medical professionals that in June 2001, the American Medical Association (AMA) spoke out against the use of antibiotics in feed given to livestock. The AMA stated that it is "opposed to the use of antimicrobials at non-therapeutic levels in agriculture, or as pesticides or growth promoters, and urges that non-therapeutic use in animals of antimicrobials (that are also used in humans) should be terminated or phased out based on scientifically sound risk assessments."

Hormones

If you are a woman, you know the power of hormones. Women are especially sensitive to the effects that fluctuating levels of estrogen, testosterone, and progesterone can have on the body, from altering menstrual cycles, to influencing menopausal symptoms (e.g., hot flashes, irritability, mood swings, bloating), to increasing the risk of certain cancers, including breast, ovarian, and uterine cancers. The body produces a certain amount of each of these hormones, and women have the option to take additional hormones, if needed, for certain purposes, including birth control and treatment of menopausal symptoms.

Unwelcome Hormones. Yet what happens if you unknowingly ingest hormones on a regular basis in the foods you eat, hormones you neither want nor need? What effect can they have on you? This is a question that has not yet been answered definitively. Some studies suggest these unwelcome hormones can cause young girls to enter puberty as young as age eight or nine or can increase the risk of breast cancer in older females. Yet the Joint Expert Committee on Food Additives reported in 1999 that giving estradiol (a type of estrogen), progesterone, and testosterone to cattle—to increase their growth rate and provide better profits for producers— poses no risks to consumers. While that thought may be the prevailing one in the United States, the European Union had already questioned the safety of hormone- treated meat and banned its importation in 1989.

Hormone-treated beef is common in the United States. Two-thirds of the 36 million-plus beef cattle in the United States are injected with growth hormones to help them bulk up. The FDA has approved six kinds of steroid hormones for use in cattle and sheep: estradiol, progesterone, testosterone, zeranol, trenbolone acetate, and melengestrol acetate. The first three are natural sex hormones; the latter three are synthetic hormone-like chemicals. All of these hormones are not effective in hogs or poultry and so are not used in these animals. One more hormone, a protein called recombinant bovine growth hormone, or rBGH, is given to dairy cows to increase milk production.

Testing for Hormones in Food. The FDA checks for residue levels of zeranol, trenbolone, and melengestrol in treated animals and has set what it considers to be a safe tolerance level for each one. However, because these natural sex hormones are made naturally by cattle and sheep, the FDA does not monitor their levels in meat animals. Studies indicate that if correct hormone treatment and slaughter techniques are used, the hormone levels in meat and milk may be higher in treated than in untreated animals, yet the levels fall within what is considered to be a safe range.

The trouble is, experts don't yet know enough about the effects of hormones in foods to say that eating treated foods is safe. We don't know, for example, if the risk of breast cancer for women who eat meat or drink milk from hormone-treated animals is greater than the risk for women who consume products from untreated animals. Such studies would require not only verifiable groups of women who do not eat foods from treated animals, but also many years of observation, because cancers typically take years to develop.

Recombinant Bovine Growth Hormone. Scientists at the FDA have concluded that eating foods that have slightly higher levels of rBGH will not have negative effects on human health. This is so, they say, because rBGH is a protein that is digested in the human body, and also because this hormone is not recognized as a hormone by human cells.

There is, however, another concern about rBGH: It triggers cells to make chemicals called growth factors. One growth factor in particular, called insulin-dependent growth factor-1 (IGF-1), is found in slightly higher levels than normal in milk from rBGH-treated cows. Studies show that women with breast cancer have higher levels of IGF-1 in their blood than women without breast cancer. So far, however, there has not been enough research to state that the IGF-1 in milk increases the risk of breast cancer in women.

ENVIRONMENTAL CONTAMINANTS

Polychlorinated Biphenyls

Polychlorinated biphenyls (PCBs) are a class of 209 different man-made, odorless compounds that belong to the category of organochlorines (see "Organochlorines" in chapter 2). Some PCBs were once used as pesticides but they have been banned from manufacture in the United States since 1977. Yet they are still found in water, soil, and food. Why are PCBs still a problem?

One reason is that they are very stable; they break down very slowly, and can exist for many decades in the environment, especially in the sediment in lakes and rivers. Thus some of the PCBs in the environment today are leftovers from the 1970s. Another reason is that disposal of PCBs was, and in some cases continues to be, done illegally or incorrectly. Leakage of PCBs into the water, air, and soil occur through illegal dumping of hazardous waste, poorly regulated toxic waste sites, and leaks from old fluorescent light fixtures and appliances made before 1978 and electrical transformers that contain PCBs.

Thus traces of PCBs can still be found in foods in the United States that have been exposed to contaminated soil and/or water. Some of the foods tainted with PCBs include fish and waterfowl (e.g., ducks, geese), and to a lesser extent, milk, eggs, dairy products, and poultry fat. The FDA requires that all these foods, plus baby food, contain no more than 0.2-3 parts per million (ppm) of PCBs, levels the FDA considers to be safe for human consumption.

Ingestion of PCBs can cause an acne-like skin condition and liver damage; they may also cause cancer and neurobehavioral changes in children. Studies show that pregnant women who ate PCB-contaminated fish gave birth to infants with motor skill problems.

Mercury

The largest threat from mercury contamination in food sources is in fish. Women who are pregnant or breastfeeding and young children should be most concerned about mercury, because the nervous systems of a developing fetus, infant, and young child can be harmed by even low levels of mercury. We explore the impact of mercury contamination and steps to minimize it in detail in chapter 12.

Dioxins

Dioxins, or DCLs, are pollutants that can be found in the soil, air, and water. Most of the dioxins in the environment come from the incineration of industrial materials which are spewed into the air, but forest fires also produce them. Dioxins build up in fatty tissues of animals that ingest contaminated water and feed and can be found in meat, poultry, fatty fish, and whole milk.

According to a study (2001) at the University of Texas School of Public Health at Houston, Americans get 22 times the maximum dioxin exposure suggested by the EPA through food alone. (Studies show that vegans—people who do not eat any animal products—have much lower levels of dioxin.) Among breastfed infants, the level can be as high as 65 times the recommended exposure. To reduce your exposure to dioxins, the Institute of Medicine suggests that everyone reduce their intake of fat from animal sources. This is especially important for women and girls, as there is evidence that dioxins can pass through the placenta of pregnant women and also taint breast milk. Young girls should begin to protect themselves years before they become pregnant by watching their fat intake from animal products. In fact, the Institute recommended to the Department of Agriculture that skim and low-fat milk instead of whole milk be served in schools to help reduce exposure to dioxins. It also suggested that the government work with farmers and food manufacturers to reduce dioxin levels in animal feed. This includes the feed fed to fish on fish farms, as researchers have found that farmed fish contain higher levels of dioxin than wild fish.

Harmful effects from dioxins can include neurological

disorders, behavioral problems, immune system disorders, and cancer. In fact, dioxins are listed as known human carcinogens.

IF YOU MICROWAVE

Remember when fast-food restaurants used foam containers, and then they switched to paper? One reason for the switch was concern for toxins that leak into the food from the containers when food is microwaved. The combination of high heat, fat, and plastics releases cancer-causing dioxins into the food and thus into your body. Instead of foam or plastic, use tempered glass, Corning Ware, or other ceramic containers to heat or cook food in a microwave.

Other Industrial Contaminants in Food

Various other industrial contaminants can also be in your food. The following is a list of some of those contaminants, which are known as volatile organic compounds, or VOCs. Although the level of VOCs in foods is generally very low, it is important to remember that you need to be concerned about the cumulative effect of ingesting these and hundreds of other toxins every day of your life. Thus every effort you make to avoid or reduce your intake of foods that have been tainted with pesticides, hormones, antibiotics, or other contaminants is a step toward better health. (You can learn which foods may have VOCs in Part II, where we talk about the FDA's Total Diet Study.)

- Benzene: One of the top 20 chemicals produced in the United States, it is a carcinogen. It is made from petroleum and used to make other chemicals such as styrene, and is also used to manufacture gasoline, rubber, dyes, drugs, pesticides, and detergents. Most exposure is through the air, but it is found in food and water as well. Ingestion of high levels of benzene in food can cause vomiting, convulsions, dizziness, stomach irritation, and coma.

- Chloroform: Causes cancer in laboratory animals and may be a human carcinogen. Chloroform can damage the liver and kidneys.
- Styrene: Used in the manufacture of plastics and rubber, it is also found in vehicle exhaust, cigarette smoke, drinking cups, and carpet backing. Styrene is a carcinogen and also can affect the nervous system by causing depression, muscle weakness, fatigue, and problems with concentration.
- Tetrachloroethylene: A chemical used in dry cleaning and metal degreasing. The International Agency for Research into Cancer says this agent is "probably carcinogenic." It is widely dispersed in the food chain and is largely found in fatty foods, such as meats and dairy products.
- Toluene: A gasoline additive, toluene is also used in leather tanning and the production of rubber and paint. Exposure can cause headache, confusion, and memory loss. It is not classified as a carcinogen.
- Xylene: One of the top 30 chemicals produced in the United States, xylene is a solvent used in the printing, rubber, and leather industries. It can cause headache, dizziness, confusion, and balance problems. Its ability to cause cancer is not known.

Acrylamide: A Non-Additive

In 2002, the FDA began assessing the risks associated with a substance called acrylamide, an ingredient commonly found in water but which recently (2002) was discovered in many foods, and at higher than expected rates. (Acrylamide appears in water because it is an ingredient in polyacrylamide, a substance added to drinking water to help purify it.)

Technically, acrylamide is not a food additive; it forms as a result of unknown chemical reactions that occur during high-temperature baking or frying of carbohydrate-rich foods, such as potatoes and corn chips. However, it is one of the substances the FDA looks for in the Total Diet Study (see details in Part II). For that reason, we explore acrylamide in this chapter.

In late 2002, scientists in the United States as well as Canada, England, Switzerland, and Australia found that foods containing high amounts of the amino acid asparagine, when heated (baking, frying, roasting), react with sugars to form acrylamide.

Acrylamide does not appear in foods before they are cooked; high-temperature cooking apparently causes the sugar in certain carbohydrate-rich foods to stick to proteins to form acrylamides. When the Center for Science in the Public Interest (CSPI) conducted some tests on French fries bought at fast-food restaurants and frozen fries from supermarkets, they discovered extremely high levels of acrylamide. The EPA has set a safe limit of 0.12 micrograms per serving (8 ounces) of water; but in the French fries, the CSPI researchers found levels of 39 to 82 micrograms per serving. Fried snacks like corn chips and potato chips were found to contain up to 25 micrograms per serving.

Boiling or steaming foods does not cause a significant amount of acrylamide to form, because water prevents sugars from binding to the proteins. Acrylamide is formed during traditional cooking techniques; thus organic foods are affected as well as conventionally produced foods.

Because acrylamide has only recently been discovered in foods, the FDA has not yet determined what health impact, if any, it may have on human health. Tests in laboratory animals show that acrylamide causes cancer, and thus it has the potential to cause cancer in humans as well. Acrylamide is known to cause nerve damage in people who have been exposed to very high levels of this substance in their work environment (acrylamide is used to make polyacrylamide, which is used in food packaging materials, plastics, grouting agents, and cosmetics).

While studies are currently underway to identify its

risks, the FDA has not issued any warnings to consumers about whether to avoid foods high in acrylamide. Some scientists, however, believe individuals should eliminate such foods. For now, the foods with the highest levels of acrylamide appear to be French fries, potato chips, corn chips, and tortilla chips; some breakfast cereals, crackers, and cookies appear to have lower levels.

BOTTOM LINE

Our food supply has become a dumping ground for additives: from waxed apples to burgers with antibiotics and hormones to ice cream with gums and artificial flavors to corn chips and French fries with acrylamides. Nearly all the additives and contaminants found in our food today didn't exist a hundred years ago. Some say the intentional additives have improved our food selection and that the unintentional ones are relatively harmless. Yet as food manufacturers have "played" with our food more and more, we have seen a parallel increase in many health problems: cancer, attention deficit disorder, food allergies, asthma, diabetes, autism, and autoimmune disorders, to name just a few.

Are additives to blame? Some experts believe that they play a significant role. The truth is, these additives and contaminants are not *natural,* and so the body has to deal with these foreign substances—typically dozens of them every day of every year—in ways experts often don't yet understand. Experts also don't know what happens in the body when you mix dozens and even hundreds of additives together. And it is apparent that the effects are an even bigger concern among the very young and the very old.

The bottom line is, avoid additives and contaminants whenever possible. Buy whole, unprocessed foods when they are available. In addition to your supermarket, visit a food cooperative, natural food store, or farmers' market in your area. Stay away from foods that contain the additives listed in the section "Should You Worry About

Food Additives?" If you eat meat, poultry, milk, or dairy foods, purchase organic products. Instead of eating fried foods and snacks such as French fries and corn chips, choose baked potatoes and pretzels. Always read labels before you buy a product. You have a choice; additives don't need to be a part of your diet.

CHAPTER 5

Genetically Modified Foods

How many genetically modified foods did you eat today? None, you say? If you ate anything that contained corn or soy in any form, such as ground corn, corn syrup, soy powder, or soy flour, you probably ate genetically modified ingredients and didn't even known it. That's because about two-thirds of the processed foods available in supermarkets contain soybeans in some form, and most soybeans are genetically altered. High fructose corn syrup, used in soda, candy, cereals, and many other products, is often made from genetically modified corn.

But you're not alone; the majority of Americans aren't aware that the supermarket shelves are filled with products that contain genetically altered ingredients, and for good reason: Food labels don't tell you they're in there.

While Americans routinely consume genetically modified corn and soybean products found in literally thousands of food items, most consumers abroad have refused to eat them. Why? Because, they say, too little is known about the possible effects these foods can have on our health and even on our genetic makeup. Scientists are anxious to get more and more genetically modified foods onto the market (for reasons we will discuss below), while those who oppose these foods try to remind the general public that all of us are guinea pigs in a vast experiment—and no one asked for our consent to participate in it. While proponents claim there's no proof that altered foods are harmful, opponents point out that no one has proved them to be safe.

So which is it? Are genetically modified foods safe for your family or not? In this chapter we will tell you what is known—or claimed—so far on this topic, and then let you decide for yourself. Because the truth is, there is no definitive answer at this time. Much more research needs to be done, and long-term studies need to be conducted. But genetically modified foods are in your refrigerator and pantry and in restaurants at this very moment, and so you should know what they are and that you have a choice to accept them or not.

WHAT ARE GENETICALLY MODIFIED FOODS?

The phrase "genetically modified (GM) food" or "genetically modified organism (GMO)" refers to plants that have been modified in the laboratory to enhance desired characteristics, such as improved nutritional value, better resistance to pests, or longer shelf life. Perhaps you remember the Flavr Savr tomato, a genetically modified tomato that was approved by the US government—against the advice of the scientists who created it—and introduced to the marketplace in February 1996. The scientists were concerned about results of tests in which rats fed the tomato developed stomach lesions. Fortunately, consumers were not impressed with the Flavr Savr (apparently many complained it had no flavor), and it was soon pulled from stores.

The Flavr Savr tomato is an example of a genetically modified food that got some publicity. The same can't be said about the other genetically modified foods that are in our markets.

Are You Eating Genetically Modified Foods?

It's true that you won't see an array of genetically modified fruits and vegetables in your neighborhood su-

permarket. But at least one genetically modified plant
has made its way into the majority of American consumers' shopping carts in a big way, and most people don't
even know it. Since 1996, when altered corn and soybeans were first introduced to consumers (without our
knowledge), the number of foods that contain genetically
modified ingredients has skyrocketed. And here's why.
The majority of processed foods contain some form of
the soybean, such as soy powder, meal, lecithin, protein,
or oil. In the United States, 81 percent of the soybean
crops are genetically modified, so chances are you're
eating lots of modified soy in products that include ice
cream, yogurt, canned tuna, salad dressings, cereals,
canned pastas, cookies, bread, and mayonnaise.

Another major modified crop is corn: 40 percent of
the corn grown in the United States is genetically modified, and corn-derived ingredients are used in thousands
of food items. Corn comes in many disguises, including
dextrose, maltodextrin, citric acid, and lactic acid, as well
as more easily identified forms such as corn starch, corn
syrup, corn meal, and corn oil.

If you eat squash or papaya, you may be eating a genetically modified food. In 2002, 54 percent of the papaya
crop in Hawaii (the only state in the United States that
grows this fruit) was genetically modified. Both yellow
squash and zucchini (green squash) have been modified
genetically, although very few farmers grow them. In addition, 54 percent of the canola crops (from which canola
oil is made) have been genetically modified.

Soon you may see many other altered foods as well.
According to the FDA and the US Department of Agriculture, more than 40 plant varieties have met the federal
requirements for genetically modified plants to become
commercially available. Some of them include sugar
beets that are resistant to herbicides; cantaloupes and
tomatoes that have had their ripening characteristics
modified; and, the one that will have the most impact on
US consumers, wheat.

How Genetic Modification Is Done

To genetically modify a plant, scientists transfer genes from one plant or organism to another plant. For example, genetically modified corn has Bt genes *Bacillus thuringiensis*, from a bacterium that produces proteins that are deadly to insect larvae. When Bt genes are transferred into corn (inserted into corn DNA), it allows the corn to produce its own lethal insecticide against pests like the corn borer. In the case of soybeans, the giant chemical company Monsanto created modified soybeans by transferring genes from bacteria, viruses, and petunias into soybean DNA. This alteration allows the modified beans to survive extensive applications of a weed killer called Roundup, which Monsanto makes. Now farmers can spray as much Roundup as they need to kill weeds, and their soybean plants survive. Soybeans that have not been modified to withstand this herbicide are choked out by the weeds and die.

Who Regulates Genetically Modified Foods?

The creation of genetically modified plants has opened up several new doors for three different government agencies that have some say in if, when, and how genetically modified foods reach consumers. The EPA is in charge of analyzing altered plants for environmental safety. Thus the herbicide-resistant soybeans (Roundup beans) and the Bt corn grown in the United States are regulated by the EPA because they involve substances that could harm the environment. The US Department of Agriculture decides if a modified plant is safe to grow, such as those created to be drought or disease tolerant, or crops grown as animal feed. The FDA evaluates whether a modified plant is safe to eat. Because the FDA traditionally has regulated food products and additives but not whole foods, it would have jurisdiction over, say, a can of tomato puree that contained genetically modified tomatoes, but it would not have authority over a whole, genetically modified tomato.

Are Genetically Modified Foods Safe?

The safety of genetically modified foods is an area of huge debate and controversy, as you'll see below when you read what proponents and opponents have to say about these foods. The FDA, whose mandate is to promote "honest and fair dealings with consumers," insists that genetically modified foods are essentially the same as natural, unmodified foods. Yet dozens of countries, especially in Europe, have banned genetically modified foods. (Some are discussing allowing such foods, but with the stipulation that they are labeled.) In essence, people in other nations are watching to see how, over time, consumption of genetically modified foods by Americans affects our health. Because the first altered foods entered the market in 1996, it may take many years for obvious or significant changes to be noticed. However, some changes, such as increased allergic reactions among children, may already be occurring, as discussed below in "What Opponents Say about Genetically Modified Foods."

Even though government agencies and the creators of genetically modified foods insist these foods are safe, many Americans would like to know which products contain altered ingredients so they can make their own decision about whether they want to feed these products to their family. The FDA insists that producers of reconstituted orange juice label their products with the words "made from concentrate," yet the agency has decided that telling consumers that a food contains untested, genetically modified ingredients isn't necessary.

This breach of the FDA's stated purpose to promote "honest and fair dealings with consumers" has led many people to insist on labeling of altered foods. In June 1999, Mothers for Natural Law (a nonprofit, activist group) presented members of Congress with nearly half a million signatures from Americans who wanted to see labels on altered foods. An October 2003 poll by the Food Policy Institute found that 94 percent of Americans think genetically modified ingredients should be labeled. Yet despite these opinions and the efforts of many activists and groups, including the Campaign to Label Genetically Engineered Foods, modified foods remain unlabeled.

If food manufacturers have their way, genetically modified foods will never be labeled. That's because they fear consumers will stop buying their products if they know they contain altered ingredients. In fact, polls have shown that the majority of Americans say they will not buy products that have been genetically modified. The questions then become, Do you have the right to know if the food you buy has the potential to cause harm and the right to make your own decisions about buying such foods? and, Is it ethical for the food industry to continue to hide possible dangers from the public?

Some food manufacturers, however, proudly label their products "GMO free." Producers of natural or unprocessed foods, such as Fantastic Foods, Nasoya, Lightlife, Yves, Cascade Farms, Eden Foods, and Annie's Naturals, for example, make sure the soybeans, soy products, corn or corn products, and canola they use come from nonmodified crops (see Appendix).

Genetic modification can be viewed as a positive or negative occurrence, depending on your perspective, as you'll see below when you read what proponents and opponents to genetically modified foods say.

What Proponents Say about Genetically Modified Foods

As the population in the United States and the world continues to grow, it's apparent we're going to need an increasing supply of food. Yet there are millions of people in the world today who are starving, and so even current food production does not meet the need.

Genetically modified foods are the answer, say advocates, because scientists can create new types of crops that can resist many of the things that reduce food production today. These super crops, they claim, will accomplish what traditional crops cannot. For example:

- Resist insect pests. To fight off crop-damaging insects, farmers typically apply tons of chemical pesticides each year. But if plants are engineered to fight off pests on their own, theoretically those insecticides won't be necessary, farmers will save money by not buying those chemicals, and they may see a bigger profit margin.

- Tolerate herbicides. Removing weeds by hand isn't feasible for most conventional farmers, so they spray large quantities of different herbicides. This is expensive and time-consuming. Genetically modified crops, like the Monsanto Roundup-resistant soybeans discussed above, are highly tolerant of the herbicide and so thrive while the weeds around them die. Advocates say that farmers of these modified soybeans need to apply only a limited amount of herbicide, so they save money and time, and also reduce the impact on the environment.

- Tolerate frost. An unexpected frost can destroy crops; thus plants that have been modified to resist frost would be welcome to farmers. Scientists have already transferred an antifreeze gene from cold-water fish into potatoes and tobacco, although these crops are not yet available to the public.

- Resist disease. Plants that could resist specific diseases that are caused by bacteria, fungi, and viruses could potentially save many crops from failure.

- Tolerate drought. Many crops are lost to drought today, and in the future the demands for irrigation water will be even greater. Thus plants created to be drought tolerant could be of great benefit.

- Improve nutrition. Although malnutrition is a global problem, it is especially critical in many third-world countries. Proponents of genetically modified crops say that if they could modify a staple crop, like rice, to contain additional nutrients, they could help improve nutrition and eliminate diseases caused by poor diet. A "super rice" has been created by researchers at the Swiss Federal Institute of Technology's Institute for Plant Sciences. This rice contains a high amount of vitamin A, a deficiency of which causes blindness in many third-world countries. However, due to opposition to genetically modified foods in Europe, this special rice is not available yet.

• Administer vaccines. This may be the most unusual use of genetically modified foods—specially created vegetables that contain vaccines. Scientists are working on modified potatoes and tomatoes that will contain vaccines and thus eliminate the need for the injectable form.

The first four of the above listed advantages of genetically modified foods are of special interest to farmers because they seem to promise higher yields and bigger profits. The environment could be another winner, because farmers should need to apply fewer pesticides, which means less runoff into the water supply and less contamination of the soil and air. Consumers also should be winners, say advocates, because produce will have less pesticide residue.

But some recent studies are not proving these advantages to be true, or at least are raising questions about them. Study results released in November 2003 by the Northwest Science and Environmental Policy Center show that use of pesticides in the United States has increased by 73 million pounds since US farmers began to grow genetically modified crops in 1996. The researchers found that farmers need to apply greater amounts of herbicides on soybeans (the Roundup-resistant variety), because the weed species are adapting to the genetically modified crop and thus are harder to control.

In a survey released in November 2003 by the Leopold Center for Sustainable Agriculture, investigators interviewed about 800 farmers in Iowa and found that farmers who grew genetically modified crops did not experience any significant difference in profits. In fact, farmers who grew modified soybeans had a smaller yield per acre than farmers who grew nonmodified soybeans. Among corn growers, yields for genetically modified corn was slightly better than the nonmodified corn, but farmers of modi-

fied corn had to spend an average of ten dollars more
per acre on seed than the other farmers. The bottom line
was that farmers who grew modified corn earned less
than four dollars more per acre than farmers of nonmodified corn.

What Opponents Say About Genetically
Modified Foods

The number one criticism of genetically modified foods
is the lack of proof that they are safe for human consumption. Many medical and scientific experts have
stated that too little is known about genetically modified
foods for anyone to make that claim. The FDA relies on
the biotech companies that create genetically modified
products to decide if their goods are safe for the marketplace. Since these same companies are vehemently opposed to labeling modified foods, it seems clear that they
will not voluntarily pull the plug on their own profit-
making products.

No one is testing to see if any particular "dose" of
genetically modified foods affects people in any way. The
creators of genetically modified foods are not officially
testing their products on people, yet everyone who unknowingly eats genetically modified foods is a guinea
pig—but without his or her consent. Yet because altered
foods are not labeled, anyone who suffers unusual health
effects has no way to prove that their symptoms are related to genetically modified foods, because none of the
foods are labeled.

When you look at the reasons why many people are
opposed to genetically modified foods, you see a common theme: concern for safety and health. Here are some
of those reasons:

- Unintended injury to other life forms. Every organism in the web of life is connected, either directly
  or indirectly, with other life forms. So when we introduce alien, genetically modified organisms into
  an ecological system, changes are bound to occur.

One such change appears to be happening already with monarch butterfly caterpillars and Bt corn. A study published in *Nature* showed that pollen from Bt corn caused monarch butterfly caterpillars, which are beneficial insects, to die. Unfortunately, Bt toxins can indiscriminately kill many different species of insect larvae, including those that are helpful to farmers. It is feared that many other negative impacts on other organisms are possible.

• Reduce effectiveness of pesticides. Insects can develop resistance to pesticides, and so some experts fear that insects will become resistant to crops that have been modified genetically.

• Cross-pollination. It appears that plants engineered to be herbicide tolerant may cross-pollinate with weeds and thus result in "super weeds," which will be resistant to the herbicide as well. In addition, some farmers have claimed that cross-pollination has occurred between their nonmodified crops and a neighboring farm's genetically altered crops.

• Allergies. An increasing number of children are developing life-threatening allergies to peanuts and other foods, and some opponents of genetically modified foods are afraid that transferring genes or other organisms into another plant may create a new allergen or cause an allergic reaction in some people. This possibility alone is a good reason, many feel, to label genetically modified foods.

BOTTOM LINE

American consumers continue to be guinea pigs in a huge experiment involving genetically modified foods. When these altered foods were first introduced to the marketplace, virtually no one in the general public knew about them. Many people argue that if the government and the biotech companies had nothing to hide, why did they sneak these products into the supermarkets? If the

FDA *really* is dedicated to promoting "honest and fair dealings with consumers," why aren't genetically modified foods labeled so consumers can make informed choices about them?

Some people believe that the only way to help protect yourself and your family against the unknowns of genetically modified foods is to choose nonmodified foods whenever possible. Buying organic foods is one way to do this. It's also necessary to speak up: Let your legislators and industry leaders know that you want altered foods labeled; that you oppose genetically modified foods; and/or that you want controlled tests to be conducted. Organizations that help you take action are listed in the Appendix.

CHAPTER 6

Irradiated Food

When you mention the word "irradiation," most people think of nuclear energy, radioactivity, or the X-rays they get at the doctor's office. Few people think about irradiation and food in the same sentence, yet some of the items in the supermarket—and in your kitchen—have been subjected to irradiation, a process whereby foods are exposed to extremely high levels of gamma rays or high-energy electrons. These energy beams are used to penetrate selected foods in an attempt to inactivate the DNA of disease-causing organisms and thus make the foods, at least theoretically, safer to eat.

We say "theoretically" because, like the genetic modification of foods, much is still unknown about possible health impacts of irradiation. Irradiation has advocates as well as opponents, with experts on both sides of the issue making claims about its safety and effectiveness. You, as a consumer and perhaps as a parent, should familiarize yourself with this topic, especially because there is a strong effort by the government to increase the number and distribution of irradiated foods, including the sale of irradiated meat to schools as part of the National School Lunch Program.

In this chapter we'll introduce you to what is known and claimed about irradiation of foods and how this method to reduce foodborne pathogens may affect you and your family. In the end, it will be up to you to decide whether irradiation is something you feel comfortable with or not.

WHAT IS FOOD IRRADIATION?

According to the Centers for Disease Control and Prevention (CDC), the irradiation of food "is a promising new food safety technology that can eliminate disease-causing germs from foods" and "can kill bacteria and parasites that would otherwise cause foodborne disease." To accomplish this, foods such as wheat flour, potatoes, and eggs are exposed to massive amounts of irradiation (the equivalent of 10 to 150 million chest X-rays, depending on the food being treated) in facilities that are surrounded by very thick concrete walls to make sure none of the rays escape. Similar technology is used to sterilize medical instruments and devices that are implanted in the body to help eliminate the risk of infection.

Food irradiation has been approved as safe and effective by the World Health Organization, the Food and Drug Administration (FDA), the US Department of Agriculture, and the CDC. It has gotten the nod for use on various food products for decades, yet most Americans are not aware of this. Here's a list of foods, when approval was granted by the FDA, and why irradiation is used:

- 1963: Wheat flour, to control mold.
- 1964: White potatoes, to inhibit sprouting.
- 1986: Pork, to kill parasites.
- 1986: Spices, herbs, and vegetable flavorings, to kill molds, bacteria, and yeasts.
- 1986: Fruits and vegetables, to control insects and increase shelf life.
- 1990: Poultry, to reduce bacterial contamination.
- 1997: Meat, to reduce bacterial contamination.
- 2000: Fresh eggs, to reduce bacterial contamination.

Although the FDA has approved irradiation for all these products, currently only a small percentage of them actually are irradiated. One exception is the spice category. More than 65 million pounds of irradiated spices are used in the United States each year. Because these products are often contaminated, they must be "cleaned" before they are added to the many products in which they are used. This is especially critical for processed meats, which are excellent breeding grounds for molds, bacteria, and yeasts. The alternative to irradiation of spices and herbs is fumigation with ethylene oxide gas, which is less effective, causes environmental concerns, and reduces flavor and color of many spices and herbs.

In October 2002, the USDA approved the importation of irradiated fruits and vegetables, which opened the door for many types of treated produce to enter the United States, including mangoes, papaya, pineapple, tomatoes, bell peppers, lychees, and sweet potatoes from Hawaii, and items from countries that have irradiation facilities. But when it comes to foods in the United States, irradiation is not common. Less than 5 percent of the beef is treated, and even fewer fruits, vegetables, and eggs. Why?

Irradiation in the United States

There are several reasons why irradiation isn't used more frequently in the United States. Some say it's because the word "irradiation" has such a negative connotation that the general public is afraid of irradiated food. Irradiation brings to mind the fear of cancer (from too much exposure to radiation) or radiation-related accidents such as the ones that occurred at Three Mile Island and Chernobyl. Many opponents of food irradiation, which include average consumers, medical professionals, and scientists, are actively trying to educate the public about the risks of food irradiation as well as influence lawmakers and food industry representatives to halt food irradiation.

Others say the food, supermarket, and food service industry executives are hesitant to bring irradiated foods to stores, restaurants, and other places that serve food because they are afraid consumers won't buy it, both because of the perception of irradiation and because it will cost slightly more. This may not be an unrealistic fear: In a CDC poll conducted in 1998–99, only about 25 percent of people said they would pay more for irradiated ground beef or poultry. In a survey done by the Food Marketing Institute, results showed that from 1998 to 2000, the percentage of consumers who said they would buy irradiated food declined from 79 percent to 38 percent.

Irradiated Foods in Schools

Although the polls and surveys indicate that Americans aren't ready to embrace irradiated foods, the US government has other ideas. In May 2003, the government approved the sale of irradiated beef to schools for the National School Lunch Program, a program that feeds low-income, disadvantaged children across the country. This decision was made even though many parents, teachers, and even children protested directly to the government. Many schools have already said they will not purchase irradiated beef, while others are unsure. What is certain is that according to federal law, irradiated meat sold to schools does not have to be labeled as such. Thus parents are being denied their right to know what their children are eating in school.

Whether the fears and concerns about food irradiation are valid is something you can decide for yourself, as we explain what the opponents and proponents of food irradiation say. We give the arguments of the opponents first, so you will understand why the proponents respond the way they do.

WHAT OPPONENTS OF FOOD IRRADIATION SAY

Consumer advocate groups like the national nonprofit Public Citizen, as well as other organizations and individuals, are working hard to educate people about the known and potential dangers of food irradiation, and questioning some of the claims made by proponents. Here are the arguments made by opponents.

Lack of Adequate Testing

Although irradiation of at least a few foods has been around for decades, there is a serious lack of studies of the long-term health effects of eating irradiated food. As opponents point out, nearly all the research on health dangers associated with irradiation was done before 1980 and it did not use modern testing methods. Rather, it was based on animal testing, which showed many cases of serious health problems such as kidney damage, reproductive problems, tumors, low birth weight, chromosome abnormalities, and shortened life span.

Then in 1980, the FDA changed how it would decide if irradiation was safe: Instead of animal testing, which is the accepted scientific approach, it used a theoretical calculation of risk based on the number of potentially harmful new chemicals consumers might encounter when eating irradiated food. The FDA formed the Bureau of Foods Irradiated Foods Task Group, which reviewed 441 studies of irradiated foods and found 32 that indicated negative effects and 37 that "appeared" to support the safety of irradiation. The rest of the studies were deemed to be inadequate. Only 5 of the 37 possibly positive studies were accepted by the Task Group. The Committee Chair Marcia van Gemert stated that "studies of sufficiently high quality to support the safety of irradiated foods . . . for long-term use are not available." Yet the FDA continues to approve the use of food irradiation.

Irradiation Creates Dangerous Compounds

Although irradiation of food does not cause it to become radioactive, something else does happen. When you treat food with the equivalent of up to 150 million chest X-rays, the molecular structure of the food changes.

Some scientists note that new and potentially dangerous
elements called radiolytic products are created when irradiation breaks apart the chemical bonds in food. Samuel
Epstein, MD, professor emeritus of Environmental and
Occupational Medicine, University of Illinois at Chicago
School of Public Health, and chairman of the Cancer
Prevention Coalition, warns that irradiation of meat
causes "profound chemical changes" that include raised
levels of the cancer-causing chemical benzene along
with radiolytic products, "some of which have been im-
plicated as carcinogenic." One group of new chemicals
produced by irradiation, known as cyclobutanones, has
been shown to cause chromosomal damage in the intestinal cells of humans and rats. (Dr. Epstein's full statement can be seen at www.organicconsumers.org/irrad/
epsteinopedl.cfm)

Irradiation Destroys Nutrients

Although advocates of food irradiation say the nutritional quality of food is not affected by irradiation, opponents claim the opposite. Research shows that irradiation
destroys up to 95 percent of vitamin A in chicken, 86
percent of vitamin B in oats, and 70 percent of vitamin
C in fruit juice. Some experts claim that irradiation can
also reduce the amount of essential amino acids and fatty
acids in food. Dr. Epstein notes that "irradiation results
in major losses of vitamins, particularly A, C, E, and the
B complex" and that these losses are increased significantly when the foods are cooked, which leaves, in essence, food that has little or no nutritional value.
Irradiated eggs, for example, have less vitamin A and
niacin than nonirradiated eggs.
Even the World Health Organization has produced
some evidence. According to a WHO report, irradiated
potatoes that are stored for six months have 50 percent
less vitamin C when compared with nonirradiated, stored
potatoes. In another WHO study, investigators found a
50 percent reduction in thiamine in irradiated codfish.

Irradiation Does Not Destroy All Disease-Causing Organisms

In the August 2003 issue of *Consumer Reports*, an article revealed the results of testing irradiated uncooked ground beef and skinless "chicken tenders." Investigators found that while the levels of bacteria in these two products were "generally much lower" than levels seen in non-irradiated meat, the treated meat still contained some bacteria. The article also pointed out that irradiated meat can still become contaminated if it is handled incorrectly after it has been irradiated, such as cross-contamination with other foods, improper storage, or inadequate cooking. Thus labels on irradiated meat and poultry must still tell consumers how to handle and cook the food properly to avoid food poisoning.

Irradiated Food Tastes and Looks Different

This is a point that both sides agree on somewhat. Professional taste testers for *Consumer Reports* noted a distinct odd taste and smell—which they likened to singed hair—in most of the irradiated beef and chicken samples they tested. In the ground beef samples, the testers could still detect the strange taste when eating the meat with a bun, ketchup, and lettuce.

Irradiated eggs don't look any different from nontreated eggs on the outside, but when you crack them, you'll see that the whites are more runny and milky than nonirradiated eggs. This can make them less effective in some recipes, especially when baking.

Irradiation Avoids the Real Problem

Critics of food irradiation, especially of meat and poultry products, say that this method takes the focus off the real problem: contamination of food in feedlots, slaughterhouses, food processing plants, cafeterias, restaurants, and other places where meat is handled and prepared. The way to reduce foodborne illnesses, they say, is to clean up food production and handling processes. Irradi-

ation is like applying a Band-Aid, which may fall off or
allow in all sorts of contaminants.

WHAT PROPONENTS OF FOOD IRRADIATION SAY

The most common analogy used to describe food irradiation is pasteurization, like the pasteurization of milk
or juices. In fact, proponents of food irradiation want to
use the phrase "cold pasteurization" instead of "irradiation" because pasteurization is a familiar, almost com-
forting term that has been accepted by the public for
years. Proponents of food irradiation believe a change in
terminology will help their cause. Changing the words,
however, doesn't change what the process does or
doesn't do to food. Those who support irradiation have
the following arguments.

Eliminates Disease-Causing Organisms

According to the CDC, use of food irradiation on approved foods, such as meat and poultry, can reduce or
eliminate disease-causing organisms. This is especially
critical, because foodborne diseases affect millions of
people and cause the deaths of thousands every year.
Thus the deadly *Escherichia coli* O157:H7 that contami-
nates beef, the salmonella and campylobacter found in
poultry, the listeria that affects processed meats like hot
dogs and deli meats, and the shigella that is found in
some fresh produce could be significantly reduced. It
could also be used to treat animal feeds, which are often
tainted with bacteria like salmonella.

Increases Shelf Life

Because irradiation reduces or eliminates harmful organisms, it can also extend the shelf life of foods. This
in turn can increase profits for food producers and allow
foods to stay "fresh" longer during shipment (especially
helpful for produce that is shipped across the country
or imported).

Maintains Food Quality

Although opponents of food irradiation claim otherwise, advocates say that the process does not cause significant changes in nutritional value or taste. In fact, the CDC says that "the changes induced by irradiation are so minimal that it is not easy to determine whether or not a food has been irradiated."

Advocates say that high doses of irradiation can cause minimal nutritional losses, which are about the same as those that occur with freezing or cooking of foods, but not the high losses that opponents claim. When it comes to taste, irradiation advocates say that most treated foods taste the same, and any minor changes that occur depend on the type of food, the irradiation dose, and the temperature during treatment. They say that many fruits and vegetables are not affected by low-dose irradiation, although dried fruit may become soft. Meat and poultry undergo little or no flavor change when irradiated at approved levels. Milk and dairy products do develop an off-taste when treated even at low doses, so these foods are not irradiated.

SHOULD YOU BUY IRRADIATED FOODS?

When it comes to irradiated meats and poultry, experts with *Consumer Reports* say there's no reason to buy them if you cook the non-irradiated forms thoroughly. According to the article, "irradiation actually destroys fewer bacteria than does proper cooking."

If, however, meat is undercooked, you are protected a bit more if the meat has been irradiated, but the risk of getting a foodborne illness is still not eliminated.

If you do buy irradiated beef or poultry, it should have a label depicting the international symbol of irradiation, a "radura," with words such as "treated with irradiation."

Produce that has been irradiated should be labeled as well, either individually or with a sign above or next to the treated items in the produce section. However, the number of irradiated fruits and vegetables on the market is very limited at this time, so knowing whether to choose treated produce may not be a question you will have to ask yourself very often. Yet if the studies showing that irradiation reduces the nutritional value of food are true, then it seems like a good idea to avoid treated fruits and vegetables. Irradiation also does not excuse you from thoroughly washing your produce, as well as storing and preparing it properly, to avoid illness, so there seems to be no reason to purchase treated produce over non-treated fruits and vegetables.

As mentioned above, irradiated eggs may have a different consistency and thus may change how they react in a recipe for, say, a cake or pudding. Again, there is no guarantee that an irradiated egg can't cause a food-borne illness.

BOTTOM LINE

Many questions about the health effects of irradiated food remain unanswered. Chief among them is, while few people may disagree that eating irradiated food on rare occasions will have much effect on health, no one really knows what the cumulative effects will be. If an increasing number of irradiated foods become available and you add them to your diet, this may become a significant concern. Also unanswered is the effect that combining irradiated foods with genetically modified foods and pesticide-contaminated foods may have on your health.

The best answer seems to be to buy and eat clean, whole foods, whether that means purchasing organic foods whenever possible (organic foods are not irradiated) or choosing conventionally grown or produced foods that are the least contaminated. In any case, be sure to wash your produce and always use the safest methods for handling and storing your foods. We talk about these topics in Part II.

You can learn more about food irradiation and ways to stop irradiated foods from being fed to our school children by contacting some of the organizations listed in the Appendix.

PART II

What's for Dinner?

CHAPTER 7

How We Know What We Know

When I was a child, I remember how my mother would cut out the recipe and a picture of the completed entrée from the magazine they appeared in and set them next to the serving dish on the table. We never needed to ask, "What's for dinner?" because it was spelled out for us. My mother wanted everyone to know exactly what they were eating.

Today, when you serve dinner to your family or you order a meal at a restaurant, do you know exactly what you're getting? If you've prepared the meal yourself, you know where you purchased the items and how they were stored and cooked. When you eat out, you must trust that the food is of good quality and that everyone who handled it did so properly.

In either situation, there are still many unanswered questions you could have about your food. Are there any contaminants on the food? Were the fruits and vegetables cleaned properly to help remove pesticide residues, and were they handled and stored in ways that help them retain their nutritional value and safety? If meat, poultry, fish, and/or eggs are part of the menu, were they handled and cooked in ways that prevent foodborne illnesses? Do any of the items contain ingredients that have been genetically modified or irradiated?

DO YOU WANT TO KNOW?

The fact that you're reading this book means you want to be informed about your food. Perhaps you've done some research on the Internet or read articles about food safety. Maybe you've seen survey results showing how other people feel about the quality of their food. According to survey results like those below, the majority of people are concerned and *do* want to know what's happening with the food supply. Here are just a few results from some recent surveys:

- In May 2003, a survey conducted by Synovate and commissioned by Whole Foods Market found that approximately 75 percent of Americans are concerned about the presence of antibiotics in the beef and poultry supplies in the United States, yet less than 50 percent are aware that the animals that provide these products are routinely given such drugs in their feed.
- In 2001, the Center for Science in the Public Interest (CSPI), conducted a survey and found that 76 percent of people wanted to know if their food has been treated with pesticides. Unfortunately, government and industry haven't followed consumers' desires for labeling of pesticide-treated foods.
- In December 2000, a report by the Pesticide Action Network of North America and Commonweal (who analyzed data from the FDA) revealed that Americans typically experience 63 to 70 separate exposures to various food-related pollutants daily. The most pervasive contaminants are DDE and dieldrin, both of which have been banned in the United States since the 1970s but which are still found in the environment. The ten most contaminated items are, in alphabetical order, butter, cantaloupe, cucumbers/pickles, meat loaf, peanuts, popcorn, radishes, spinach, summer squash, and winter squash.
- In February 1999, about 66 percent of American adults questioned during a national survey did not

know that supermarkets sell genetically altered foods. Yet 81 percent of all the soybeans grown in the United States have been genetically modified, as well as 40 percent of the corn. This is very significant, as both of these products are found in thousands of food items, including breakfast cereals, salad dressings, cake mixes, frozen dinners, baby food, and beverages, in the form of soy protein, soy powders, soy flour, corn syrup, corn meal, corn starch, and other items.

Do you want to know more about the food you feed your family? If you do, Part II of this book will help you. You'll learn about foods in eight different categories: fruits and vegetables, cereals and grains, beans and soy, meat, poultry, fish, dairy and eggs, and oils and fats. You'll learn how to choose the healthiest and safest foods in each group, how to recognize those that may not be safe, and how to store and prepare the foods. The information you gather from these chapters will be invaluable to you when you go to the supermarket and shop for your family.

WHERE WE GOT THE INFORMATION

Much of the information in Part II was collected from various sources, including the Food and Drug Administration (FDA), which has two programs from which we gleaned data: the Total Diet Study and the pesticide monitoring program of domestic and imported foods. We also gathered information from the US Department of Agriculture (USDA) and its Pesticide Data Program; two nonprofit, consumer/public advocacy groups—the Pesticide Action Network of North America and the Environmental Working Group, both of which analyze government data for consumers—and data published in various scientific journals.

Total Diet Study

The FDA's Total Diet Study identifies levels of contaminants and nutrients in the foods Americans eat. The program was initiated in 1961 to monitor for radioactive contamination of foods related to nuclear testing. Since then the study has undergone many changes, and today it analyzes levels of pesticide residues, industrial chemicals (PCBs and VOCs), other toxic substances, and nutrients in prepared foods—for example, in apple pie instead of just apples alone. It does not, however, look for every possible contaminant; for example, it doesn't look for bacteria that can cause food poisoning.

Four times a year, the FDA sends employees to purchase foods in supermarkets in selected cities across the United States. The samples are prepared (e.g., apples are used in apple pie; ground beef is made into meat loaf; frozen fish sticks are heated) and then analyzed. The results of the latest Total Diet Study for which results are available (2001) show that analysts tested 1,030 food items and found 107 individual residues. A list of the top 19 pesticides detected and the percentage of samples that contained them is below in Table 2.

If you have an infant, you will probably be especially interested in the results of a separate analysis of 78 samples of baby food that was done as part of the Total Diet Study. Results of that analysis are also below in Table 3. (You should know that the pesticide residue levels in all the samples analyzed in the 2001 Total Diet Study were below tolerance; that is, at levels deemed to be safe by the FDA when consumed individually.)

Table 2
Pesticide Residues Found in Prepared Foods

Pesticide	Percentage of Samples (Of 1,030 Total Samples)
DDT	23
Chlorpyrifos-methyl	20
Endosulfan	18

Pesticide	Percentage of Samples (Of 1,030 Total Samples)
Malathion	16
Dieldrin	15
Chlorpropham	7
Chlorpyrifos	7
Permethrin	6
Carbaryl	5
Iprodione	4
Dicloran	3
Heptachlor	3
Lindane	3
Hexachlorobenzene	3
Thiabendazole	3
Methamidophos	2
Acephate	2
Methoxychlor	2
Quintozene	2

Table 3
Pesticide Residues Found in Baby Foods

Pesticide	Percentage of Samples (Of 78 Total Samples)
Carbaryl	21
Endosulfan	13
Chlorpyrifos-methyl	10
Malathion	10
Chlorpyrifos	9
Iprodione	9
Permethrin	9
Ethylenethiourea	9
Thiabendazole	6
Dicloran	3
DDT	1
Dieldrin	1
Phosmet	1
Esfenvalerate	1

FDA Pesticide Monitoring Program

The FDA's pesticide monitoring program looks for pesticide residues (but not hormones, antibiotics, drugs, or organisms associated with foodborne illness) in mostly unprepared foods, both domestic and imported, including fruits and vegetables, corn, oats, rice, soybeans, wheat, barley, milk, dairy, eggs, shellfish, and fish. The 2001 report includes information on 6,475 samples: 2,101 domestic and 4,374 imported. Overall, pesticide residues were found in 39.8 percent of domestic products and 28 percent of imported products, which suggests that our domestic food supply is not as "clean" as imported products. The FDA's program is able to detect 394 pesticides and identified 113 in its samples.

The program also found that 1.1 percent of fruits and 1.5 percent of vegetables grown domestically had pesticide levels that were unsafe. Among imported produce, 2.8 percent of fruits and 6.4 percent of vegetables exceeded the safety levels. We report on results for individual foods throughout chapters 7 through 12.

USDA Pesticide Data Program

The USDA tests thousands of samples of fruits and vegetables (both domestic and imported, fresh and processed), rice, beef, poultry, and water for pesticide residues. The report for 2001 includes the results of 12,264 analyzed samples. Overall, the investigators found that about 64 percent of fruits and vegetables had pesticide residues, and about 19 percent of beef tested positive for residues. (Remember, this report gives pesticide residues only; contamination with bacteria or other disease-causing organisms or levels of antibiotics or hormones are not reflected.) The vast majority (9,903) of the samples were fruits and vegetables.

HOW TO USE PART II

In the next eight chapters, you will read about general categories of foods and specific items in each category.

For each item, we have included information about pesticides, industrial contaminants, antibiotics, or other substances that may affect the food; tips on how to purchase, store, and/or prepare the food; and other safety tips when relevant. If you would like more information on pesticides, organically produced foods, additives, genetically modified foods, or irradiation, you are encouraged to return to Part I and read the relevant chapter(s). Periodically throughout chapters 8 through 15 you are referred to the Appendix, which contains more in-depth information on selected pesticides, how to prevent foodborne illnesses, and contact information for whole, organic foods suppliers.

CHAPTER 8

Fruits and Vegetables

You've probably seen the advertisements in magazines or the signs in supermarkets in the produce section: "5 A Day For Better Health," the mantra of the National Cancer Institute. Increasingly, health experts are urging people to eat more fruits and vegetables because these important foods come with a long list of benefits, not least of which is the fact that most of them are warehouses of vitamins, minerals, and other nutrients, plus fiber, that help maintain overall health and significantly reduce the risk of developing various cancers and other serious medical conditions. So when you choose your produce, you want it to be the best quality for you and your family.

ISSUES TO CONSIDER

Conventionally Grown or Organic?

One thing to remember as you reach for apples, bunches of spinach, or other produce is that both conventionally grown and organically grown produce can harbor pesticide residues, although the latter has significantly less. This fact has been demonstrated in many studies, including one led by the Consumer Union in 2002, in which researchers found pesticide residues on 75 percent of conventionally grown food compared with 23 percent of organically grown foods. Many people are surprised that organic foods may have pesticide residues at all. As we mentioned in chapter 3, small amounts of pesticides may find their way onto organic produce, despite the best and most law-abiding efforts of organic producers. However, organic produce is still the better deal, and here's why.

Less is best. If you buy organic fruits and vegetables, you have a significantly lower chance of getting any pesticides as part of your purchase. Even if you do, properly washing or preparing organic produce (see below) will reduce that risk even more.

In addition, the health benefits from eating a variety of fruits and vegetables every day far outweigh the risks associated with ingesting a minute amount of pesticides. And if you follow the suggestions offered in this chapter, you will reduce any risks associated with pesticides even further.

Pathogens and Foodborne Illness

Another consideration when choosing fruits and vegetables is the presence of pathogens—disease-causing organisms—such as bacteria, parasites, fungi, and molds, which can transmit foodborne diseases. One example of this occurred in late 2003, when hundreds of people who ate at a Mexican restaurant in Pennsylvania developed hepatitis A. The source of the pathogen was eventually traced to the raw green onions, imported from Mexico, served at the restaurant. In this case, as in most other cases of food poisoning, cooking the food thoroughly would have killed the contaminants. However, many people eat fruits and vegetables raw, and so this is an example of how improper handling of produce—in this case, apparently by the exporters—resulted in widespread illness.

The truth is, fruits and vegetables are susceptible to contamination by various pathogens, whether they are

grown in the United States or other countries. Any produce that is handled incorrectly—whether it is free of
pathogens when you bring it home from the market or
not, or whether it was grown conventionally or
organically—can be unsafe for you and your family.
That's why it's so important to follow simple guidelines
which we discuss in this chapter.

General Tips for Purchasing, Handling, and Consuming Produce

In addition to specific safety recommendations for individual fruits and vegetables, which are discussed later in
this chapter, here are some general guidelines for purchasing, handling, and consuming fruits and vegetables
to avoid pesticide residues and pathogens.

- All fresh produce, whether conventionally or organically grown, should be washed thoroughly (see individual fruits and vegetables for more information)
  just before serving, *not* before storing them. To
  wash produce, use cool water or, if you prefer, a
  commercial produce wash (e.g., Fit); however, most
  experts agree these offer little or no advantage over
  plain water. Do *not* use soap or chlorine, except in
  certain situations (e.g., melons; see "Cantaloupe"
  below).
- Scrub firm produce (e.g., carrots, turnips, potatoes,
  melons) with a clean produce brush (a natural bris-
  tle brush is best; plastic bristles can bruise produce),
  and wash the individual leaves of greens. Always
  rinse produce well with plain water.
- Discard the outer leaves of leafy vegetables (e.g.,
  lettuce, cabbage), because pesticide residues are
  more likely to gather there.
- Fruits and vegetables that you will peel (e.g., melons, oranges, pineapples) should be washed as well,
  because cutting into them with a knife can transfer
  pesticide residues into the pulp of the produce.
- Peel any fruit or vegetable that has been waxed (see

"Waxed Produce" in chapter 4, for more information and a list of produce that is usually waxed).

- Bacteria grow very rapidly on cut produce, so refrigerate it as soon as possible after cutting.
- If you buy bagged salads or other prepared fresh vegetables, always wash them, even if the label says they have been prewashed.
- Do not use any fruits or vegetables that are moldy, badly bruised, slimy, or shriveled. Pathogens can thrive in produce that is decaying. Minor blemishes are typically safe; in fact, organic produce, which has not been subjected to waxing and coloring and other attempts to make it look "perfect," sometimes has minor blemishes.
- Do not store greens near fruits, which give off ethylene gas and which will cause greens to develop brown spots and decay.
- To prevent bruising, always place your produce on top of your other groceries in your shopping cart, and place them on top in your grocery bags.
- Never purchase or use fruits or vegetables that are in cans that have been damaged. The most obvious sign of spoiled canned foods is a can that is swollen. The lid of the can should be slightly concave, not bulging or flat.
- Dehydrated vegetables should always be cooked thoroughly, as they are susceptible to contamination by many different microorganisms, and thus have the potential to cause foodborne illness.

HOW CLEAN IS YOUR PRODUCE?

The Environmental Working Group, a nonprofit, environmental research organization in Washington, DC, which provides information to the general public on issues of public health such as pesticides in food, environmental pollutants, and toxins in health and beauty products, has conducted several investigations into pesticide contamination of fruits and vegetables. Its latest report was published as *The Shopper's Guide to Pesticides in Produce,* and it ranked the amount of pesticide residue contamination for 46 fruits and vegetables based on an analysis of more than 100,000 tests that were conducted between 1992 and 2001 by the Food and Drug Administration and the US Department of Agriculture. You can see the complete list at www.foodnews.org/fullresults.php but we thought you should know the top ten most contaminated and the ten least contaminated fruits and vegetables. Remember: The best way for you to avoid pesticides as much as possible is to buy organic and to wash, wash, wash.

Most Contaminated	Least Contaminated
Peaches (most contaminated overall)	Bananas
Strawberries	Broccoli
Apples	Onions
Spinach	Asparagus
Nectarines	Peas
Celery	Mangoes
Pears	Cauliflower
Cherries	Pineapple
Potatoes	Avocadoes
Sweet bell peppers	Sweet corn (least)

LET'S GO SHOPPING

In this section we look at specific fruits and vegetables and offer you guidelines on how to identify and purchase the safest varieties for your family and how to store and prepare them. When we refer to the FDA's pesticide monitoring program or Total Diet Study, or to the USDA's Pesticide Data Program, we are referring to 2001 report results. For more information about various pesticides mentioned in the entries, refer to chapter 2 and the Appendix; for more on industrial contaminants, see chapter 4.

Apples

A high percentage of apples have pesticide residues. According to the FDA's pesticide monitoring program, 67.8 percent of apple samples had residues, and one sample exceeded the tolerance limit. The USDA program found 91 percent of samples to be contaminated and detected 24 different residues. Among the most common residues detected were the organophosphates azinphosmethyl and phosmet (can cause nervous system damage); diphenylamine (fungicide, not believed to be a carcinogen), and thiabendazole (likely carcinogen). The 2001 Total Diet Study also detected benomyl and endosulfan (can cause nervous system damage) and the industrial chemicals benzene (carcinogen) and toluene.

Processed Products. Apple juice, apple cider, and apple sauce contain the same pesticide residues as the whole apples from which they are made, and in some cases, additional residues as well. In the 2001 Total Diet Study, for example, analysts found residues of ethylenethiourea in applesauce and carbaryl in apple juice (as well as thiabendazole). Samples of strained apple juice for infants had traces of benzene, carbaryl, chloroform (probable carcinogen), and thiabendazole.

When buying apple juice or apple cider, get pasteurized products. There have been cases in which unpasteurized apple juice and cider were made from ground-tagged apples (apples that fall to the ground and are collected), which can have high levels of microorganisms, including potentially deadly E. coli (see chapter 1). Frozen apple juice rarely presents any health problems.

Safety Hints. If you purchase conventionally grown apples or apple products, chances are they have many pesticide residues. Wash apples with water and scrub with a produce brush. If the apples have been waxed, it is best to peel them, as wax seals in contaminants. Unfortunately, peeling apples does not guarantee that you have removed all the pesticides, as some may have entered the pulp. The safest alternative is to buy organic apples, apple cider, and other apple products. Many supermarkets now carry organic produce, but other sources are natural food stores, food cooperatives, and farmers' markets.

Look for apples that are firm; don't buy apples that have rotten spots or a brown core. Large apples are more likely to be overripe. Store apples in a cool, dry place or in the refrigerator crisper in a plastic bag. If you have room, store apples so they don't touch each other; this helps them last longer. Stored properly, apples will keep three to four weeks. Organic apples may have some slight blemishes that do not affect the quality of the fruit.

Apricots

The FDA's pesticide monitoring program found that 75 percent of domestic and 50 percent of imported apricots had pesticide residues. The Total Diet Study identified the organophosphates chlorpyrifos and malathion on its samples, as well as the carbamate carbaryl (all can cause nervous system damage), captan (probable carcinogen), and iprodione (likely carcinogen).

Processed Products. Dried apricots, apricot nectar, and apricot oil contain the same pesticide residues as do the whole apricots from which they are made. If you buy dried apricots, you should also look for ones that have not been treated with sulfur dioxide, an additive that improves shelf life and color, but which can cause allergic reactions in some people.

Safety Hints. When purchasing fresh apricots, look for fruit that is golden orange and evenly colored and plump. Ripe apricots yield to gentle pressure on the skin. Do not buy apricots that are soft or very firm, pale yellow, or that have a greenish color. You can store apricots in the refrigerator in a plastic bag, where they can keep for up to one week. Wash apricots with water before using. To further reduce your exposure to pesticides, buy organically grown apricots, which can be found in some supermarkets, but more likely in food cooperatives, farmers' markets, or natural food stores.

Artichokes

The FDA pesticide monitoring program found pesticide residues on only 5.6 percent of imported artichokes (no domestic figures were given). Some of the pesticides used on artichokes include diuron (known carcinogen), endosulfan and methidathion (can cause nervous system damage), and methyl bromide (see Appendix).

Safety Hints. Look for plump artichokes that are heavy for their size. The scales should be thick and green. Do not buy artichokes that have brown spots or gray-black discoloration on the scales. To minimize exposure to pesticides, buy organic artichokes, which may be found in some supermarkets, but more likely at farmers' markets, food cooperatives, and natural food stores.

Asparagus

According to the Environmental Working Group, asparagus are among the least contaminated of vegetables. The FDA's pesticide monitoring program found that 88.9 percent of domestic and 91.5 percent of imported asparagus were free of pesticide residues. Dicloran, a fungicide believed to be relatively nontoxic, was found in samples of the Total Diet Study.

Safety Hints. Shop for asparagus that have green stalks at least one-half inch thick with tightly closed tips. Do not buy asparagus that have flat, white, split, or woody stalks. Because asparagus lose their nutritional quality quickly, use them within one to two days after purchase.

Store in a plastic bag in the refrigerator. Before use, wash asparagus with water and squish the tops in a container of water to loosen any dirt that may lodge there. To further minimize your risk of exposure to pesticide, buy organically grown asparagus, available at some supermarkets, but most likely at food cooperatives, farmers' markets, and natural food stores.

Avocados

Avocados are among the safest fruits, says the Environmental Working Group, and results of the FDA's pesticide monitoring program seem to agree. Zero percent of domestic and only 4.5 percent of imported avocados had pesticide residues. The Total Diet Study found traces of industrial contaminants—benzene (carcinogen), chloroform (probable carcinogen), toluene, and xylene—in its avocado samples.

Safety Hints. Avocados come in different varieties, which vary in size, color, and shape. Generally, however, avocados are ripe when they are slightly soft. Look for fruit that yields to gentle pressure on the skin. If you don't plan to use them immediately, buy firm fruit that does not yield to pressure. Light brown markings on the skins usually have no effect on the flesh of the fruit. Do not buy avocados that have dark sunken spots or cracks. To ripen avocados at home, keep at room temperature for three to five days, or place in the refrigerator to slow ripening. To prevent the flesh from becoming brown once you cut the fruit, immediately place the flesh in lemon juice until ready for use.

Wash avocados before peeling them. Even though conventionally grown avocados are relatively free of pesticide residues, you can further decrease your risk of exposure by buying organically grown avocados. These are available in some supermarkets but more likely at farmers' markets, food cooperatives, and natural food stores.

Bananas

According to the FDA pesticide monitoring program, 56.6 percent of bananas (nearly all bananas available in the United States are imported from South and Central America) had pesticide residues, although, reports the Environmental Working Group, only 4.7 percent had more than one residue. Among the residues found on bananas in the Total Diet Study were thiabendazole (likely carcinogen) and the industrial contaminants styrene (carcinogen) and xylene.

Safety Hints. Shop for bananas that are firm, bright, and free from bruises. Bananas that are speckled with brown spots are ripe. Do not buy fruit that is grayish (indicates it has been exposed to cold and thus will not ripen) or bruised. Bananas with green tips will ripen at room temperature (60 to 70 degrees) over a period of a few days. If you want to extend the life of a ripe banana, refrigerate it. Although the skin will darken, the flesh should not be affected.

To further reduce your risk of exposure to pesticide residues, you can buy organically grown bananas, available at some supermarkets, farmers' markets, food cooperatives, and natural food stores.

Beets

Beets appear to be relatively safe vegetables; none of the domestic or imported samples analyzed by the FDA revealed pesticide residues. The Total Diet Study found traces of dieldrin and endosulfan (both can cause nervous system damage) in its samples.

Safety Hints. Look for beets that are round, firm, deep red, and with a smooth surface. If the greens are still attached, they should look fresh. Do not buy beets that are elongated or that have scales around the top surface. Trim the tops to one-half inch to reduce wilting. Store beets in the refrigerator in a plastic bag, where they should keep for up to two weeks.

Wash beets with water and a vegetable brush. To minimize exposure to pesticides, buy organic beets, which may be available in some supermarkets, but more likely in natural food stores, farmers' markets, and food cooperatives.

Blueberries

The FDA pesticide monitoring program found that 35.3 percent of domestic and 33.2 percent of imported blueberries had pesticide residues. Some of the pesticides approved for use on blueberries are the organophosphates chlorpyrifos, diazinon, and malathion (all can damage the nervous system), the organochlorine endosulfan (may cause birth defects, cancer, nervous system damage), captan (probable carcinogen), and diuron, iprodione, and pyrethrins (all likely carcinogens).

Safety Hints. Look for blueberries that have a dark blue color with a silvery cast, which is a natural coating. Blueberries should be firm, plump, dry, and uniform in size. Do not buy fruit that is soft or leaking juice. When you get the berries home, discard any that are too soft, moldy, or leaking. Refrigerate the remaining berries by first blotting them dry, then placing them on a shallow plate covered with a paper towel and plastic wrap. Before using blueberries, wash them in a pan of water and rinse in a colander. To further reduce your risk of exposure to pesticides, buy organically grown blueberries, which may be available at some supermarkets, but more likely at natural food stores, food cooperatives, and farmers' markets.

Bok Choy

Imported bok choy appears to be a much safer choice than domestic; the FDA's pesticide monitoring program found that 60 percent of domestic but only 5.3 percent of imported bok choy had pesticide residues. Pesticides applied to bok choy may include benomyl (to be withdrawn by 2005), carbaryl (possible carcinogen), maneb (probable carcinogen), and phosphine (can cause gastrointestinal problems).

Safety Hints. Shop for bok choy that has firm, thick, fleshy stalks and fresh, green leaves. Store it in a plastic bag in the refrigerator for one to two days. Rinse each leaf and stalk under running water and shake dry. To minimize exposure to pesticides, buy organic bok choy, which may be available at some supermarkets, but more likely at Asian food markets, food cooperatives, natural food stores, and farmers' markets.

Broccoli

According to the USDA Pesticide Data Program, 29 percent of broccoli samples had pesticide residues, and a total of 22 different agents were found. The most common pesticide found was DCPA, an herbicide that is considered to be nearly nontoxic. The Total Diet Study detected DDE, a metabolite of DDT (may cause nervous system damage, birth defects, cancer) in its samples.

Safety Hints. Look for broccoli that has firm, compact clusters of florets, which should be dark green and may have a purplish tone. Avoid broccoli that has enlarged, open, or yellowish florets. Store broccoli in a plastic bag in the refrigerator and use within three days of purchase. Before using, cut off the hard ends of the stalks and wash the remaining stalk and florets thoroughly with water. To further reduce your risk of exposure to pesticides, buy organically grown broccoli, available in some supermarkets as well as food cooperatives, farmers' markets, and natural food stores.

Brussels Sprouts

The Total Diet Study found residues of carbaryl and

chlorpyrifos (can cause nervous system damage), DDE and endosulfan (may cause birth defects, nervous system damage, cancer), and permethrin (possible carcinogen) in samples of brussels sprouts.

Safety Hints. Look for sprouts that are green with tight outer leaves and free from blemishes. Avoid those that are turning yellow. Fresh brussels sprouts should be sold under refrigeration, because room temperature causes the outer leaves to turn yellow quickly. Tiny holes in the leaves may indicate worms. Store brussels sprouts in the refrigerator in a plastic bag. They should keep for three to five days.

Wash the sprouts under running water and remove yellow or wilted outer leaves. To minimize exposure to pesticides, buy organic brussels sprouts, available at some supermarkets, but more likely at farmers' markets, natural food stores, and food cooperatives.

Cabbage

The USDA Pesticide Data Program found residues on 11.1 percent of domestic and 13 percent of imported cabbage. The Total Diet Study found no residues. Some of the pesticides applied to cabbage include captan and lindane (both probable carcinogens), ethoprop (likely carcinogen), methyl bromide (see Appendix), and the organophosphate methyl parathion (can cause nervous system damage).

Processed Products. The Total Diet Study looked at samples of canned sauerkraut and homemade coleslaw. Residues of dieldrin and endosulfan (may cause birth defects, cancer, nervous system damage) and triphenyl phosphate (can cause nervous system damage) were found in the sauerkraut, while DDT, dieldrin, lindane (likely carcinogen), and the industrial contaminants chloroform (probable carcinogen) and toluene were found in the homemade coleslaw. Some of the pesticides found in the coleslaw may have been contributed by the dressing.

Safety Hints. Store cabbage in a plastic bag in the refrigerator crisper. Remove the outer leaves of cabbage and discard them before washing the head with water. For best results, cut the head into quarters or remove the leaves individually, depending on how you want to use the cabbage, to wash them. To minimize your risk of exposure to pesticides, buy organically grown cabbage and cabbage products, which can be found in some supermarkets, as well as natural food stores, food cooperatives, and farmers' markets.

Cantaloupe

The FDA pesticide monitoring program found that 71.4 percent of domestic and 51.3 percent of imported cantaloupes had pesticide residues. Pesticides found on cantaloupe in the Total Diet Study include endosulfan and toxaphene (may cause cancer, birth defects, nervous system damage), methamidophos (can damage the nervous system), and thiabendazole (probable carcinogen).

Safety Hints. Look for mature cantaloupe, which should have no stem and a smooth, shallow indentation where the stem was. This indentation should yield slightly to light pressure, which means the fruit is ripe. The veining on the skin should be coarse and corky, and the color of the skin between the veining should be yellowish gray or pale yellow. Thumping on a melon does not identify how ripe it is. If the melon is not yet ripe, you can ripen it at room temperature for two to four days. A ripe cantaloupe can be stored in the refrigerator in a plastic bag for up to ten days. A cantaloupe is overripe if the rind is very yellow or there is softening over the entire rind.

Even though you don't eat the rind, you should wash a cantaloupe before cutting it because pesticide residues from the rind can be transferred from the knife to the flesh. You can use water and a vegetable brush, or wash the rind with a diluted chlorine bleach solution: one teaspoon of bleach in one gallon of water. Rinse the melon thoroughly. To further minimize exposure to pesticides, buy organic cantaloupe, which are available in some supermarkets, but more likely in food cooperatives, natural food stores, and farmers' markets.

Carrots

The FDA pesticide monitoring program found residues on 30 percent of domestic and 21.4 percent of imported carrots, while the USDA Pesticide Data Program found a much higher number: 81 percent with detectable pesticides, including iprodione (likely carcinogen) and DDE (may cause nervous system damage, birth defects, cancer). Traces of iprodione and DDE were also found in fresh carrots in the Total Diet Study. Samples taken of strained carrots for infants contained residues of industrial contaminants, including benzene and styrene (both carcinogens), chloroform (probable carcinogen), and toluene.

Safety Hints. Choose carrots that are a deep orange color. Avoid those that are very dark at the top end or those that have a lot of little roots or are oversized. If the tops are attached, cut them off before storing in the refrigerator. Carrots should be placed in a plastic bag and refrigerated, where they will keep for up to two weeks. Before using carrots, wash them with water and scrub with a vegetable brush. If you wash them thoroughly, peeling isn't necessary. To further reduce exposure to pesticide residues, buy organic carrots and organic strained carrots for infants, which are available in some supermarkets and at food cooperatives, natural food stores, and farmers' markets.

Cauliflower

The Environmental Working Group named cauliflower as one of the least contaminated vegetables. This finding is supported by results of the FDA's pesticide monitoring program, in which 0 percent of domestic and only 8.3

percent of imported cauliflower had pesticide residues. The Total Diet Study did detect permethrin (possible carcinogen) in its samples.

Safety Hints. Choose cauliflower that has firm, compact florets that are white and free of black spots. To store cauliflower, place it in a plastic bag and put in the refrigerator. Use within three to four days of purchase. Before using cauliflower, remove the outer leaves, cut the head into pieces, and wash thoroughly with water. To minimize exposure to pesticides, buy organically grown cauliflower, which can be purchased at some supermarkets as well as natural food stores, food cooperatives, and farmers' markets.

Celery

The Environmental Working Group has identified celery as one of the vegetables most likely to have pesticide residues. This is supported by findings of the FDA's pesticide monitoring program, which found that 83.3 percent of domestic and 52.9 percent of imported celery had residues. Pesticides found in the Total Diet Study include the organophosphates acephate and methamidophos (can damage the nervous system), dicloran, and permethrin (possible carcinogen).

Safety Hints. Fresh celery should have solid, rigid stalks and fresh or only slightly wilted leaflets. Avoid celery that has flabby upper stalks or hollow or discolored stalks. At home, you can wrap celery in aluminum foil and refrigerate it, where it should keep for several weeks.

You should wash celery with water before using it, but unfortunately pesticides can penetrate the vegetable and can't be washed away. Therefore it is recommended that you buy organic celery whenever possible. Some supermarkets may carry it, but you will more likely find it at farmers' markets, natural food stores, or food cooperatives.

Cherries

A high percentage—89 percent—of cherries were found to have pesticide residues, according to the USDA Pesticide Data Program. Among the residues were the organophosphates azinphosmethyl and malathion and the carbamate carbaryl, all of which can damage the nervous system. The FDA's pesticide monitoring program found that 67.4 percent of domestic and 66.7 percent of imported cherries had residues. Pesticide residues detected by the Total Diet Study included those already named, as well as acephate (can cause nervous system damage), iprodione (likely carcinogen), and permethrin (possible carcinogen).

Safety Hints. Buy cherries that are dark maroon to black for the richest flavor. Rainier cherries are a straw-colored variety. The best cherries are glossy, plump, and bright. Avoid cherries that are shriveled, dull, have brown spots, or are leaking. Wash cherries thoroughly with water before using. To minimize your exposure to pesticides, buy organically grown cherries. Some supermarkets may carry organic cherries, but you are more likely to find them at a natural food store or farmers' market.

Collards

Analysis by the FDA showed that 36.4 percent of domestic collards (no figures for imported) had pesticide residues. According to the Total Diet Study, residues included DDE, dieldrin, endosulfan, and toxaphene (all may cause birth defects, cancer, nervous system damage), and permethrin (possible carcinogen).

Safety Hints. Look for bright, green leaves and sturdy stems; do not buy collards that look wilted or that have yellowing leaves. Store in a plastic bag in the refrigerator crisper, where they should keep for several days. Separate the leaves and wash each separately. To minimize exposure to pesticides, buy organic collards, which may be available in some supermarkets, but more likely at farmers' markets, natural food stores, and food cooperatives.

Corn

Sweet corn, which is the type we eat most often, has been rated the safest type of produce, according to the Environmental Working Group. Results of the FDA's pesticide monitoring program concur, as it found no residues on domestic corn and traces on only 4.2 percent of imported corn. Field corn, which is fed to livestock and is used to make items such as corn grits, corn oil, and cornmeal, may be contaminated with aflatoxin, a naturally occurring mold that is known to cause cancer in laboratory animals (see chapter 8).

Although corn appears to be a relatively safe food choice, it is treated with some very toxic pesticides, including alachlor and diuron (both likely carcinogens), captan and mancozeb (both probable carcinogens), methyl bromide (see Appendix), and disulfoton (can cause nervous system damage), among others.

Besides contamination with pesticides or aflatoxin, another consideration with corn is the fact that 40 percent of the crop grown in the United States is genetically modified (see chapter 5). Depending on how you feel about genetically modified foods, you may want to look for corn products that are labeled as being made with non-GM corn.

Processed Products. The Total Diet Study looked at samples of canned cream corn and found the industrial contaminant chloroform (probable carcinogen). Items such as corn flakes, corn chips, and popcorn are made from sweet corn, while corn grits and cornmeal are made from field corn. All of these products are discussed in chapter 8, "Grains and Grain Products," under the entry for corn.

Safety Hints. When buying corn on the cob, look for fresh husks that have silk ends free from decay and fresh stem ends. The kernels should be plump, yellow or white, but not too large. Avoid ears that have very large kernels, wilted or dried husks, or discolored or dry stem ends. Corn keeps best if you keep the husks on and refrigerate it immediately, in a plastic bag, as soon as you get it home. It should keep two to four days.

The husks protect the kernels from contamination; however, once you remove the husks, you should still wash the ears with water before preparing. Boil the ears for at least three to five minutes. Although corn is considered to be very safe, you can further minimize any risk by buying organic corn and corn products, which will also eliminate your exposure to aflatoxins and genetically modified products.

Cranberries

The FDA pesticide monitoring program found that 60 percent of domestic and 0 percent of imported cranberries had pesticide residues. Some of the pesticides approved for use on cranberry crops include the organophosphates acephate, azinphosmethyl, chlorpyrifos, and malathion and the carbamate carbaryl (all of which can cause nervous system damage) and the probable carcinogens folpet and maneb.

Processed Products. You can expect to find the same pesticide residues in cranberry sauce and cranberry juice as you do in the fresh cranberries from which they are made.

Safety Hints. Look for plump, firm berries with a bright color. Some varieties of cranberries are dull, but they still should be red. Avoid brown or discolored berries or those that are spongy or leaky. Wash cranberries thoroughly with water in a pan and rinse with water in a colander. To minimize exposure to pesticides, buy organically grown cranberries. Some supermarkets may carry organic cranberries and cranberry products, but you are more likely to find them at a natural food store, food cooperative, or farmers' market.

Cucumbers

According to the FDA's pesticide monitoring program, 36.8 percent of domestic and 58.3 percent of imported cucumbers had pesticide residues. Residues detected in the Total Diet Study included endosulfan and dieldrin (may cause birth defects, nervous system damage, cancer) and methamidophos (can cause nervous system damage).

Processed Products. The Total Diet Study looked at dill cucumber pickles and found residues of dieldrin, endosulfan, permethrin (possible carcinogen), and toxaphene (can cause birth defects, cancer, nervous system damage).

Safety Hints. Look for cucumbers that are green and firm over the entire length. Avoid cucumbers that are large in diameter, turning yellow, or with shriveled ends. Conventionally grown cucumbers are usually waxed, which seals in pesticides. Wash and then peel cucumbers before eating them. To further minimize exposure to pesticides, buy organic cucumbers, which are available in some supermarkets but more likely at farmers' markets, food cooperatives, or natural food stores.

Eggplant

Analysis by the FDA showed that 20 percent of domestic and 36.7 percent of imported eggplant had pesticide residues. The Total Diet Study found evidence of endosulfan (may cause birth defects, nervous system damage, cancer) and methamidophos (can cause nervous system damage) on its samples.

Safety Hints. Shop for a well-rounded eggplant that has a satiny smooth skin, even coloring, and bright green stems and caps. It should feel heavy for its size. Avoid eggplant that is poorly colored, soft, or wrinkled. Eggplant will keep in a plastic bag in the refrigerator crisper for up to three to four days. Because this vegetable bruises easily, store it with that in mind.

Wash eggplant with water and peel it before use, as most eggplant has a wax coating that seals in pesticide residues. Unfortunately, some pesticides may be in the flesh, but cooking eggplant may help reduce those levels. To further minimize exposure to pesticides, buy organic eggplant, which may be available in some supermarkets, but more likely in farmers' markets, food cooperatives, or natural food stores.

Endive

Analysis by the FDA revealed that 66.7 percent of domestic and 9.1 percent of imported endive had pesticide residues. Some of the pesticides applied to endive include carbaryl, diazinon, dimethoate, and methyl parathion (all can cause nervous system damage) and maneb (probable carcinogen).

Safety Hints. Belgian endive is a small, cylindrical head of pale, tightly packed leaves. Curly endive has green-trimmed, curly leaves; escarole has broad, pale green leaves. In all cases, buy crisp, firm heads. To store endive, wrap the head in a paper towel and place it in a plastic bag in the refrigerator crisper. It should keep for two to three days. Before using, separate the leaves and wash thoroughly with water. To reduce your exposure to pesticides, buy organic endive, which may be available at supermarkets, as well as food cooperatives, natural food stores, and farmers' markets.

Grapefruit

The FDA pesticide monitoring program reported that 80 percent of domestic and 33.2 percent of imported grapefruit had pesticide residues. Pesticide residues discovered in the Total Diet Study include carbaryl (can cause nervous system damage) and thiabendazole (likely carcinogen).

Processed Products. Grapefruit juice can be expected to have the same pesticides as those on the fruit from which it was made. According to the Total Diet Study, however, samples of grapefruit juice made from frozen concentrate showed traces of ethion, a pesticide that may cause birth defects.

Safety Hints. Buy firm fruit that is heavy for its size. Grapefruit that is thin-skinned tends to be juicier than thick- or coarse-skinned fruit. Defects on the skin, such as scars, discoloration, or scratches, rarely affect the taste of the fruit. Avoid fruit that has soft spots. Even though you don't eat the rind, you should wash grapefruit with a vegetable brush and water before you cut it with a knife, because residue from the rind can be transported into the flesh on the knife. To minimize exposure to pesticides, buy organic grapefruit and grapefruit juice, both of which may be available at some supermarkets, but more likely at farmers' markets, natural food stores, and food cooperatives.

Grapes

According to the FDA pesticide monitoring program, 25 percent of domestically grown grapes and 63.4 percent of imported grapes had pesticide residues, while the USDA Pesticide Data Program found pesticides on 73 percent of grapes. The most significant residues found included captan (probable carcinogen), which was detected in both the Total Diet Study and the USDA study, and iprodione, a likely carcinogen.

Processed Products. Grape juice, grape jelly, and grape jam, as well as wine, can be expected to contain the same pesticide residues as the grapes from which they were made. Samples from the Total Diet Study found carbaryl (causes nerve damage) and iprodione in jelly and juice, and carbaryl in juice. Dry wine samples contained carbaryl, dicloran (believed to be relatively nontoxic), and iprodione. Raisins, which are dried grapes, are discussed in their own entry (see "Raisins" below).

Safety Hints. Several varieties of grapes are available, but generally you want plump fruits that are firmly attached to the stem, which should be mostly green and bendable. Green or white grapes are sweetest when they have a yellowish color and a tinge of amber. Red grapes are best when they are all or mostly red. Avoid grapes that are soft or wrinkled or those that are on a brown, dry stem.

Store grapes in a plastic bag in the refrigerator. They generally keep for up to two weeks, but it is best to eat them within two to three days to minimize the growth of bacteria. Do not wash grapes until you are ready to eat them. Wash them thoroughly with water and rinse with water in a colander. Peeling grapes can help reduce the amount of pesticides you ingest, but it isn't practical. Unfortunately, some pesticides invade the flesh of grapes and can't be removed by washing. To best minimize your exposure to residues, buy organic grapes and grape products, which may be available at some supermarkets, but more likely at farmers' markets, natural food stores, and food cooperatives.

Most wine makers add sulfites to their products to help preserve them, and the label should state that these substances have been added. This information is important if you are susceptible to sulfites. If you want to avoid pesticides in your wine, consider organic varieties. Organic wines are available from several sources (see Appendix).

Green Beans (Snap Beans)

The USDA Pesticide Data Program revealed that 62 percent of green beans had pesticide residues, including the organophosphates acephate and dimethoate, and the organochlorine endosulfan. All of these pesticides can cause damage to the nervous system. The FDA pesticide monitoring program reported more reassuring figures; it detected residues in 22.4 percent of domestic and 35.7 percent of imported green beans. Like the USDA report, the Total Diet Study found acephate and endosulfan residues in its samples, but it also found iprodione (likely carcinogen).

Processed Products. Both acephate and dieldrin (which causes nervous system damage) were found in samples of strained green beans for infants.

Safety Hints. Look for beans that have vivid color and a velvety feel and firm texture. The beans should snap crisply when broken. Do not buy beans that have bulging seeds. Store green beans in a plastic bag in the refrigerator crisper, where they should keep for three to five days.

Wash beans with water and gentle hand rubbing before use. To further minimize exposure to pesticides, buy organically grown beans. Some supermarkets, food cooperatives, natural food stores, and farmers' markets may carry organic green beans.

Honeydew

The FDA pesticide monitoring program found that 100 percent of domestic and 61.9 percent of imported honeydew had pesticide residues. Some of the pesticides approved for use on honeydew include captan (probable carcinogen), DCPA (believed to be relatively nontoxic), methyl bromide (see Appendix), and fenvalerate (may damage the nervous system).

Safety Hints. A good honeydew has a yellowish white to creamy rind that has a velvety texture, a slight softening at the blossom end of the fruit, and a faint fruity aroma. Avoid fruit that has a white or greenish white rind and a hard, smooth feel.

Even though you do not eat the rind, you should wash

the fruit before you cut it, because pesticide residues can be transferred on the knife to the flesh. Use a produce brush and water to clean the rind. A chlorine bleach/water solution (one teaspoon of chlorine to one gallon of water) can also be used to clean the rind. To further minimize your exposure to pesticide residues, buy organically grown honeydew. Some supermarkets may carry them, but you are more likely to find them at farmers' markets, food cooperatives, and natural food stores.

Kiwi

The FDA pesticide monitoring program found that 0 percent of domestic and 15 percent of imported kiwi had pesticide residues, making them a relatively safe fruit. Some of the pesticides approved for use on kiwi include the organophosphates chlorpyrifos, diazinon, pirimiphos-methyl, and phosmet (all of which can damage the nervous system) and the likely carcinogen iprodione.

Safety Hints. Buy unwrinkled, plump fruit that is firm or yields slightly to the touch. Kiwi is fully ripe when it yields to light pressure but is not soft. To ripen kiwi, leave it at room temperature for a few days. Do not buy fruit that is starting to shrivel or that is very soft.

The outer skin is edible, but it is best to peel conventionally grown kiwi before eating them. Kiwi should be washed with water and rubbed gently. To minimize exposure to pesticides, buy organic kiwi. Some supermarkets may carry organic kiwi, but you are more likely to find them at food cooperatives, natural food stores, or farmers' markets.

Lemons

The FDA pesticide monitoring program reported that 100 percent of domestic and 50 percent of imported lemons had pesticide residues. Some of the many pesticides approved for use on lemons include aldicarb and malathion (both can damage the nervous system), and methyl bromide (see Appendix).

Processed Products. Lemonade may contain the same pesticide residues as the lemons from which it is made. The Total Diet Study, however, did not find any residues in samples of lemonade made from frozen concentrate.

Safety Hints. Look for lemons that are firm, heavy for their size, and with a rich yellow color. The skin should be relatively smooth, as a rough skin indicates the fruit has little flesh. Avoid lemons that have hard or shriveled skin, mold, soft spots, or a dull or darker yellow color. Store lemons in a sealed plastic bag in the refrigerator, where they should keep for several weeks, or at room temperature for several days.

Although most lemons have pesticide residues, their thick skins help protect you against ingesting the contaminants. However, you should wash the lemon rind with a vegetable brush and water because cutting into the lemon with a knife can transfer residues into the flesh. To further minimize your risk of ingesting contaminants, you should buy organically grown lemons, especially if you are using lemon slices for iced tea or lemon peel (zest) for recipes. Some supermarkets, but more likely food cooperatives, farmers' markets, and natural food stores, may carry organic lemons.

Lettuce

According to the USDA Pesticide Data Program, 49 percent of lettuce samples had pesticide residues, including the highly toxic DDE. The FDA pesticide monitoring program reported similar figures: 43.3 percent of domestic and 56.2 percent of imported head lettuce had pesticide residues. Leaf lettuce (e.g., red leaf) fared better: 26.1 percent of domestic and 22.7 percent of imported leaf lettuce had pesticides. Types of pesticides found in head lettuce sampled in the Total Diet Study were benomyl (to be withdrawn by 2005), endosulfan (may cause

birth defects, cancer, nervous system damage), and thiabendazole (probable carcinogen).

Safety Hints. When shopping for head (iceberg) lettuce, look for a solid head that has medium green outer
leaves and lighter green or pale green inner leaves.
Avoid head lettuce that is very hard or that has hard
bumps on top, which indicates an overgrown central core.
Leaf lettuce should have broad, tender leaves that are
not wilted. Slight discoloration of the tips of leaf lettuce
usually doesn't affect the quality, but avoid lettuce that
has serious color changes.

Store lettuce in a plastic bag in the refrigerator crisper.
Iceberg usually keeps about two weeks; romaine, ten
days; and leaf lettuces, four days. When preparing lettuce, remove the outer leaves and wash the rest of the
head or leaves with water, separating the leaves to make
sure you wash each one. Unfortunately, some pesticide
residue can penetrate the leaves and cannot be removed
with washing. To minimize your exposure to pesticides,
buy organically grown lettuce, which is often found in
supermarkets, as well as in natural food stores, farmers'
markets, and food cooperatives.

Limes

The FDA pesticide monitoring program found that 0
percent of domestic and 0 percent of imported limes had
pesticide residues. Some of the pesticides that are applied
to limes include aldicarb and malathion (both of which
can damage the nervous system), and methyl bromide
(see Appendix).

Safety Hints. Shop for limes that are heavy for their
size and that have a glossy skin. Avoid limes that have
soft spots or dull, dry skin. Store limes in a sealed plastic
bag in the refrigerator, where they should keep for several weeks, or at room temperature for several days.

Although limes appear to be a safe fruit, to further
minimize your exposure to pesticide residues you can

buy organically grown limes, which may be available in some supermarkets, but more likely in farmers' markets, natural food stores, and food cooperatives.

Mangoes

The FDA's pesticide monitoring program found that 19.8 percent of imported mangoes had pesticide residues (no figures on domestic fruit). Some of the pesticides used on mangoes include captan and lindane (probable carcinogens), ferbam and thiabendazole (likely carcinogens), malathion (can cause nervous system damage), phosphine (can cause gastrointestinal disturbances), and methyl bromide (see Appendix).

Safety Hints. Mangoes come in several varieties and colors. Look for mangoes with skin that has a blush of yellow-orange or red. When mangoes are ripe, they yield to slight pressure and have some black speckles. Too many speckles, however, may indicate damaged flesh. To ripen mangoes, place two in a paper bag (or if you have only one mango, put an apple or banana in the bag). Once ripe, store in the refrigerator, where it should keep for two to three days.

Wash and peel mangoes before eating. To reduce your exposure to pesticides, buy organic mangoes, which may be in some supermarkets, but most likely in natural food stores, food cooperatives, and farmers' markets.

Mung Bean Sprouts

Mung bean sprouts appear to be relatively safe; the FDA's pesticide monitoring program found that 0 percent of domestic and only 14.3 percent of imported sprouts had pesticide residues. Two pesticides approved for use on mung bean sprouts are trifluralin and 4-chlorophenoxyacetic acid (neither believed to be carcinogenic).

Safety Hints. Mung bean sprouts are available in plastic bags, loose in a basin of water, or in clear containers so you can evaluate their quality. Look for crisp sprouts that smell clean. Do not buy sprouts that are slimy, discolored, or have a sour smell. Once at home, refrigerate the sprouts and make sure they are loosely packed. Bagged sprouts usually keep about three days, while boxed sprouts may last four or five. Rinse them thoroughly in a colander before use.

To minimize exposure to pesticides, buy organic sprouts, which may be available in supermarkets, but more likely in farmers' markets, natural food stores, and food cooperatives.

Mushrooms

The FDA pesticide monitoring program found that 0 percent of domestic and 0 percent of imported mushrooms had pesticide residues. The Total Diet Study, however, reported traces of thiabendazole (likely carcinogen) as well as dimethoate and diazinon (can cause nervous system damage) on its samples. Thiabendazole and diazinon were also found by analysts with the USDA Pesticide Data Program, which noted that 66 percent of its samples had residues.

Safety Hints. Look for mushrooms with caps that are either closed around the stem or that are open slightly with pink or light tan gills. The top of the cap should be creamy or white, or a light brown, depending on the type of mushroom. Avoid mushrooms that have discolored or damaged caps.

Mushrooms are 90 percent water, so proper storage is important to prevent them from going bad. Store in a paper bag in the refrigerator crisper; never use plastic, because it traps moisture and turns mushrooms slimy. To clean mushrooms, wash using water and a wet cloth or a mushroom brush, available in kitchen supply stores. To minimize exposure to pesticides, buy organic mushrooms, which may be available in some supermarkets, but more likely at farmers' markets, food cooperatives, and natural food stores.

Mustard Greens

Fifty percent of domestic and 20 percent of imported mustard greens had pesticide residues, according to the FDA's pesticide monitoring program. Some of the pesticides applied to mustard greens include captan, maneb, and lindane (probable carcinogens), iprodione (likely carcinogen), endosulfan (may cause birth defects, nervous system damage, cancer), and parathion (can cause nervous system damage).

Safety Hints. Look for bright green leaves and sturdy stems; do not buy mustard greens that look wilted or that have yellowing leaves. They will keep for several days if stored in a plastic bag in the refrigerator crisper. Separate the leaves to wash them. To minimize exposure to pesticides, buy organic mustard greens, which may be available in some supermarkets, but more likely at farmers' markets, natural food stores, and food cooperatives.

Nectarines

The USDA Pesticide Data Program reported that 97 percent of nectarines had pesticide residues, including the organophosphate phosmet (can cause nervous system damage) and propargite (probable carcinogen). The FDA pesticide monitoring program found pesticide residues on 66.7 percent of domestic and 100 percent of imported nectarines.

Safety Hints. Shop for nectarines that are plump and slightly soft along the "seam." Avoid hard, dull, soft, or shriveled fruit. Bright, firm fruit will ripen within two or three days at room temperature. Once ripe, refrigerate nectarines, where they should keep for up to one week. Some staining of the skin will not detract from the quality of the fruit. To minimize your exposure to pesticide residues, buy organic nectarines, available at some supermarkets, but more likely at farmers' markets, food cooperatives, or natural food stores.

Okra

Zero percent of domestic and 19.3 percent of imported okra showed evidence of pesticide residues, according to the FDA's pesticide monitoring program. Pesticides applied to okra include carbaryl (possible carcinogen), lindane (probable carcinogen), malathion (can cause nervous system damage), and methyl bromide (see Appendix). The Total Diet Study found evidence of dimethoate (can cause nervous system damage).

Safety Hints. Shop for pods that are tender, bright green, free of blemishes, and less than four inches long. Do not buy okra that is pale, hard, or that resists bending. Okra placed in a paper or plastic bag in the refrigerator crisper should keep for up to three to four days. Wash with water and use a vegetable brush to remove the "fuzz" from the pods.

To minimize your exposure to pesticides, buy organic okra, which will most likely be found at natural food stores, farmers' markets, and food cooperatives.

Olives

The FDA's pesticide monitoring program reported that 100 percent of olive samples tested were free of pesticides. No results were available for domestic olives. The Total Diet Study found residues of 2-chloroethyl linoleate and 2-chloroethyl palmitate (which can damage the nervous system), and DCPA (believed to be relatively nontoxic) on its black olive samples.

Processed Products. Olive oil can be expected to contain the same pesticides as the olives from which it is made. See more about olive oil in chapter 14.

Safety Hints. Both green olives (which are picked unripe) and black olives are considered safe fruits. If you want to minimize your risk of pesticide exposure, you can purchase organic olives, which may be available from some natural food stores as well as online (see Appendix).

Onions

Onions and family members are among some of the safest vegetables. The FDA pesticide monitoring program found that 0 percent of domestic and 14.8 percent of imported onions, scallions, and leeks had pesticide residues. Some of the pesticides applied to these vegetables include the organophosphates azinphos-methyl and malathion (cause nervous system damage), captan and maneb (probable carcinogens), chlorothalonil and cypermethrin (likely carcinogens), and methyl bromide (see Appendix).

Safety Hints. Choose yellow, red, or white onions that are firm or hard and dry and relatively free of blemishes. Avoid onions that have soft necks or with fresh sprouts. When choosing scallions or leeks, look for those with crisp, green tops; avoid those that are wilted, discolored, or yellowing. Onions should be stored in a cool, dry, dark area, while scallions and leeks should be refrigerated.

Peel away the outer layers of onions, scallions, and leeks to reduce your risk of pesticide exposure. Unfortunately, some residues may penetrate the flesh of the onion and cannot be removed. Cooking may reduce these contaminants. To further minimize exposure, shop for organic onions, scallions, and leeks. Some supermarkets may carry organic varieties, but you can also find them at farmers' markets, natural food stores, and food cooperatives.

Oranges

According to the FDA pesticide monitoring program, 64.3 percent of domestic and 30.3 percent of imported oranges have pesticide residues. Similarly, the USDA Pesticide Data Program found residues on 83 percent of samples. Toxins detected by the Total Diet Study included the industrial contaminants chloroform (probable carcinogen) and toluene, as well as the likely carcinogen thiabendazole.

Processed Products. Orange juice and orange marmalade typically contain the pesticides found in the oranges from which they were made. According to the Total Diet Study, residues of the pesticides carbaryl (possible carcinogen) and ethion (can cause nervous system damage), and the industrial contaminants chloroform (probable carcinogen), toluene, and xylene were detected in orange juice.

Safety Hints. Look for oranges that are firm and heavy, with bright-looking skin. Oranges that are light for their size or those that have very rough or dry, spongy skin should be avoided. Oranges typically can be stored for about one week in the refrigerator.

Even though orange rinds normally are not eaten, you should wash the fruit with water and a vegetable brush before you cut it because residues can be transferred on the knife into the pulp. To minimize exposure to pesticide residues, buy organic oranges, which may be available at supermarkets, but more likely at food cooperatives, natural food stores, and farmers' markets. If a recipe calls for orange zest (the rind), be sure to use organic oranges.

Papaya

The FDA's pesticide monitoring program reported that 0 percent of domestic and 15.8 percent of imported papayas had pesticide residues. Some of the pesticides applied to papaya include diuron (known carcinogen), mancozeb (probable carcinogen), malathion (can cause nervous system damage), permethrin (possible carcinogen), phosphine (can cause gastrointestinal disturbances), and thiabendazole (likely carcinogen).

Safety Hints. Papaya comes in several varieties. These fruit turn from green to yellow-orange as they ripen. Papaya that are completely green without a tinge of yellow may not ripen properly. They are ripe when they are 75 to 100 percent yellow or yellow-orange and the fruit gives slightly when pressed. To ripen papaya, place in a paper bag; add a banana to hasten ripening. Once ripe, papayas keep in the refrigerator for about one week.

Papayas should be washed with water and gently rubbed, then peeled. To minimize exposure to pesticides, buy organic papaya, which are available at some supermarkets, but more likely at food cooperatives, natural food stores, and farmers' markets. An additional advantage of buying organic papaya is to avoid genetically modified fruits: 54 percent of papaya produced in Hawaii (the only US state that grows papaya) are genetically modified (see chapter 5).

Peaches

According to the Environmental Working Group study, peaches are the most contaminated of the fruits: they had the most pesticides of all the fruits tested—45— and the most pesticides detected on a single sample—9. The Total Diet Study identified the organophosphates chlorpyrifos and phosmet (can cause nervous system damage) and iprodione (likely carcinogen) on its samples. The USDA Pesticide Data Program, which found only 1 percent of peaches to be free of pesticide residues, adding azinphos-methyl and several other pesticides to that list.

Processed Products. Peach jam and peach nectar typically contain the pesticides of the peaches from which they were made. These products were not specifically tested by the FDA or USDA. The Total Diet Study found residues of carbaryl and chlorpyrifos (both can cause nervous system damage) and permethrin (possible carcinogen) in samples of strained peaches for infants.

Safety Hints. Look for peaches that are fairly firm or just slightly soft. Avoid peaches that are very hard, very soft, or that have bruises. Ripen peaches at room temperature and, once ripe, keep in the refrigerator for up to one week.

Before eating, thoroughly wash peaches with water and peel them. Some pesticides may have penetrated the pulp, however, and cannot be removed with washing. To minimize your exposure to pesticides, buy organic peaches and peach products. Some supermarkets may carry organic peaches, but you are more likely to find them at farmers' markets, food cooperatives, and natural food stores.

Pears

The FDA pesticide monitoring program found that 73.5 percent of domestic and 37 percent of imported pears had pesticide residues. The Total Diet Study identified the organochlorine dicofol (may cause birth defects, nervous system damage, cancer) and the likely carcinogens iprodione and thiabendazole on its samples.

Processed Products. Samples of strained pears for infants revealed traces of ethylenethiourea, for which there is inadequate evidence for carcinogenicity.

Safety Hints. Pears come in several varieties: Bartletts are pale to rich yellow; Anjou are light green to yellowish green; Bosc are greenish yellow to brownish yellow; and Winter Nellis are medium to light green. Look for firm pears in all varieties and avoid fruit that is shriveled or that has a weakening of flesh near the stem. Hard pears will usually ripen if kept at room temperature. Ripe pears can be kept in the refrigerator for up to one week.

To minimize exposure to pesticides, buy organic pears, which may be available in some supermarkets, but more likely in natural food stores, food cooperatives, or farmers' markets.

Peas, Green Field

About 95 percent of the peas consumed in the United States are canned or frozen, but they all start out fresh. The FDA's pesticide monitoring program found that 13.5 percent of domestic and 39.2 percent of imported peas had pesticide residues. Some of the pesticides applied to peas include carbaryl (possible carcinogen); diazinon, malathion, parathion, and phosmet (can cause nervous system damage); and diuron (known carcinogen).

Safety Hints. If you buy fresh peas, look for those that are in a refrigerated area, because peas kept at room temperature lose their sugar and turn to starch within a few hours. Look for glossy, firm pods that feel velvety. Shake the pods; the peas should not rattle loosely inside. Avoid pods that are large, ready to burst, or dull. Fresh peas are best when eaten the same day they are purchased, but if you store them, do so in a plastic bag and refrigerate them for one to two days only. Do not shell the peas until you are ready to cook them. Rinse off the pods, then crack them open to remove the peas, which can be rinsed as well.

To minimize exposure to pesticides, buy organic peas, which may be available at some supermarkets, but more likely at farmers' markets, food cooperatives, and natural food stores.

Peppers

The FDA pesticide monitoring program found pesticides on 55.7 percent of domestic and 38.3 percent of imported sweet peppers. Traces of acephate and methamidophos, organophosphates that can cause nervous system damage, were found on samples analyzed in the Total Diet Study. Some of the other pesticides used on peppers include captan (likely carcinogen); diazinon, malathion, and endosulfan (can cause nervous system damage); and permethrin (possible carcinogen). The Environmental Working Group also found that of all the vegetables tested, sweet bell peppers had the most pesticides detected—39.

Although studies were not available on levels of pesticides on chili, jalapeño, and other hot peppers, these varieties are treated with most of the same pesticides as are sweet peppers.

Safety Hints. Select firm, thick-fleshed peppers that have a bright color (green, yellow, red). Avoid peppers that are blistered or that have soft flesh. Store peppers in the refrigerator crisper section for up to two weeks. Most peppers are coated with wax to help retain moisture, but it also seals in pesticide residues. Unfortunately, peppers have a very thin skin and can't be peeled when raw, but blanching allows you to remove the thin outer layer. Washing peppers with water and scrubbing with a vegetable brush can help reduce pesticide exposure, but some residues may penetrate into the pulp. When handling hot peppers, wear rubber gloves and do not touch your face with your gloved hands, as the oil from the peppers can burn.

To minimize exposure to pesticides, buy organic peppers, available in some supermarkets as well as natural food stores, farmers' markets, and food cooperatives.

Pineapple

The Environmental Working Group has named the pineapple as one of the least contaminated fruits and vegetables. Results of the FDA's pesticide monitoring program agree; it found that 0 percent of domestic and 19.6 percent of imported pineapple had pesticide residues. Some of the pesticides used on pineapple include diazinon, ethoprop, and malathion (all can cause nervous system damage); diuron (known carcinogen); lindane (probable carcinogen); and pyrethrins (likely carcinogens).

Safety Hints. Shop for fragrant, bright-colored pineapples that are heavy for their size. The "eyes" that pattern the fruit should be only slightly separated. Avoid fruit with eyes that are sunken, dark, or watery, or fruit that is discolored or has soft spots.

Store pineapples in the refrigerator or at room temperature. At room temperature, the fruit will soften but not ripen. If you cut a pineapple, wrap it in plastic or store it in an airtight container in the refrigerator, where it should keep for three to four days. Before use, wash pineapples with water and a vegetable brush. To minimize exposure to pesticides, buy organic pineapple, which are available at some supermarkets, but more likely at farmers' markets, natural food stores, or food cooperatives.

Plums

According to the FDA's pesticide monitoring program, 72.7 percent of domestic and 44.4 percent of imported plums have pesticide residues. The Total Diet Study identified chlorpyrifos (can cause nervous system damage) and iprodione (likely carcinogen) on its samples.

Processed Products. Prunes are dried plums, and so can be expected to have the same pesticide residues as the plums from which they were made. The Total Diet Study found evidence of dicofol and endosulfan (may cause cancer, birth defects, nervous system damage) and iprodione on its prune samples, as well as endosulfan in its prune juice analyses.

Safety Hints. There are more than 140 varieties of plums available in the United States. Look for plums that are fairly firm to slightly soft, plump, and well colored for the variety. Do not buy plums that have brown discoloration or that are hard or very soft. To soften hard plums, place them in a loosely closed paper bag and keep at room temperature for one to two days. When soft, refrigerate. Ripe plums should keep for up to three days in the refrigerator.

Wash plums with water before using. Peeling helps reduce exposure to pesticides, but unfortunately some toxins may penetrate into the flesh of the fruit. To further reduce your risk, buy organic plums, which may be available at some supermarkets, but more likely at natural food stores, food cooperatives, and farmers' markets.

Potatoes

The FDA pesticide monitoring program reported that 58.3 percent of domestic and 6.7 percent of imported potatoes contained pesticide residues. The USDA Pesticide Data Program found 82 percent of potatoes to have residues, including the possible carcinogen DDE and chlopropham (may cause tumors). Chlorpropham was also detected in the Total Diet Study, as were DDE, DDT, and endosulfan (may cause birth defects, cancer, nervous system damage), and chlorpyrifos (can cause nervous system damage).

Processed Products. Two of the most popular foods among Americans—French fries and potato chips—were analyzed by the Total Diet Study. It discovered that potato chips had residues of the industrial contaminants benzene and styrene (both carcinogens), chloroform (probable carcinogen), toluene, and xylene, as well as the pesticides chlorpropham and endosulfan (can cause tumors and nervous system damage, respectively). Frozen French fries contained chlorpropham and endosulfan, while those sampled from fast-food restaurants had these pesticides as well as DDE (possible carcinogen), dieldrin (may cause birth defects, cancer, nervous system damage), and the industrial contaminants styrene (carcinogen) and chloroform (probable carcinogen). Another potato product—mashed potato flakes—contained DDE and endosulfan.

Safety Hints. Choose potatoes that are firm and without sprouts or green color. Store them in a cool (45 to 50 degrees), humid, dark place with good ventilation. Properly stored potatoes will keep for up to one month.

Throw out any potatoes that become shriveled or have many sprouts. Potatoes exposed to light will turn green and produce a toxic substance. Peel off the green sections of potatoes before using them. Potatoes kept in a refrigerator will develop a sweet taste and turn brown when cooked.

Wash and scrub potatoes and then peel them before use, as pesticides concentrate in the skins. (If you buy organic potatoes, you can keep the skins on and thus get more fiber and nutrients than in peeled potatoes.) Unfortunately, some residues penetrate past the skin and cannot be washed away. To minimize your risk of exposure to pesticides, buy organic potatoes and potato products, which are available in some supermarkets, as well as natural food stores, farmers' markets, and food cooperatives.

Radishes

Fifty percent of domestic and only 5 percent of imported radishes showed evidence of pesticide residues, according to the FDA's pesticide monitoring program. The Total Diet Study identified chlorpyrifos (can cause nervous system damage) and DDE (possible carcinogen) in its samples. Some of the other pesticides used on radishes include allethrin (may affect the nervous system), the organophosphates diazinon and malathion (can cause nervous system damage), and ziram (likely carcinogen).

Safety Hints. Shop for firm, round, red radishes that are about one inch in diameter and that have fresh-looking tops (if they are still attached). Avoid large radishes or ones that appear dry or that have yellow tops. Radishes will keep for several weeks in the refrigerator crisper in a plastic bag. Wash with water and a vegetable brush before using.

To minimize exposure to pesticides, buy organic radishes, which may be available in some supermarkets, but more likely at farmers' markets, natural food stores, or food cooperatives.

Raisins

Raisins are the most popular dried fruit (grapes) in the United States. Because they start their lives as grapes, they can be expected to have the same pesticide residues as the grapes from which they are made. The FDA's pesticide monitoring program found residues on 25 percent of domestic and 63.4 percent of imported grapes/raisins. Results of the Total Diet Study found residues of DDE and dicofol (may cause cancer, birth defects, nervous system damage), propargite (probable carcinogen), and the industrial contaminants benzene (carcinogen), chloroform (probable carcinogen), toluene, and xylene.

Safety Hints. It takes four pounds of grapes to make about one pound of raisins, so any pesticides in the grapes are concentrated in the raisins. It is best to purchase organic raisins, which are available at natural food stores, food cooperatives, and some farmers' markets. Black/brown raisins are the most popular; however, if you like golden raisins, you should know that they are treated with sulfur dioxide, which cannot be tolerated by some people (see chapter 4).

Raspberries

The FDA's pesticide monitoring program found pesticide residues in 66.7 percent of domestic and 32.3 percent of imported raspberries. Some of the pesticides applied to raspberries include 2,4-D (may cause birth defects), captan (probable carcinogen), diazinon and malathion (can cause nervous system damage), dicofol and endosulfan (may cause birth defects, nervous system damage, cancer), diuron (known carcinogen), and iprodione (likely carcinogen).

Safety Hints. Shop for berries in which the individual small bulbs that make up the berry are plump and tender but not soft. Avoid leaky or moldy berries. Raspberries are very perishable. When you get the berries home, discard any berries that are too soft, moldy, or leaking. Refrigerate the remaining berries by first blotting them dry, then placing them on a shallow plate covered with a paper towel and plastic. Use within one to two days. Raspberries freeze well: Rinse and drain, spread the berries on a cookie sheet and freeze, then transfer the frozen berries into an airtight bag. Frozen raspberries will keep up to one year.

To minimize exposure to pesticides, buy organic raspberries, which may be available at some supermarkets, but more likely at natural food stores, farmers' markets, and food cooperatives.

Spinach

Sixty percent of domestic and 40.9 percent of imported spinach showed evidence of pesticide residues in the FDA's pesticide monitoring program. The Total Diet Study identified DDE, DDT, dieldrin, and endosulfan (all may cause birth defects, cancer, nervous system damage), lindane (probable carcinogen), diphenyl 2-ethylhexyl phosphate (can cause nervous system damage), and permethrin (possible carcinogen) in its samples.

Safety Hints. Shop for spinach that has fresh, young, tender leaves. Avoid spinach that has coarse or fibrous stems. Store in a plastic bag in the refrigerator crisper, where it can keep for several days. Separate the leaves and wash each separately. To minimize exposure to pesticides, buy organic spinach, which may be available in some supermarkets, but more likely at farmers' markets, natural food stores, and food cooperatives.

Squash (Summer)

Varieties of summer squash include crooked neck, pattypan, straight neck, and zucchini. The Total Diet Study found residues of dieldrin, endosulfan, and toxaphene (all may cause birth defects, cancer, nervous system damage) in samples of boiled summer squash. The FDA pesticide monitoring program found that 27.9 percent of domestic and 50 percent of imported squash had pesticide residues.

Safety Hints. Choose squash that are firm and heavy for their size. The skin should be evenly colored and slightly shiny, not waxed. Overgrown squash may be stringy and coarse. Store in the refrigerator in a plastic bag, where it should keep for up to one week.

Wash squash with a vegetable brush before using. Because many squash are waxed, which seals in pesticides, you may want to peel the vegetable after washing. Although washing and peeling summer squash helps reduce exposure to pesticides, dieldrin is absorbed into the flesh and can't be removed. To minimize exposure to pesticides, buy organically grown summer squash.

Squash (Winter)

Winter squash include acorn, butternut, buttercup, Hubbard, spaghetti, pumpkin, and banana. The Total Diet Study found residues of dieldrin and endosulfan (may cause birth defects, cancer, nervous system damage) and methamidophos (can damage the nervous system) in samples of baked winter squash. The FDA pesticide monitoring program noted that 27.9 percent of domestic and 50 percent of imported squash had pesticide residues.

Safety Hints. Choose squash that are firm and heavy for their size. The rinds should have a dull sheen, and slight variations in color will not affect the flavor. If the stem is attached, it should be round and dry. Do not wash squash before storing them. Most varieties will keep up to three months if stored in a cool, dry place. Exceptions are spaghetti squash, which will keep for two months, and Hubbard, which will last up to six months. If you cut squash into pieces, cover them with plastic wrap and refrigerate. Use within one week.

Wash squash with a vegetable brush before using. Because many squash are waxed, which seals in pesticides, you may want to peel the vegetable after washing. Although washing and peeling winter squash helps reduce exposure to pesticides, dieldrin is absorbed into the flesh and can't be removed. To minimize exposure to pesticides, buy organic squash. Some supermarkets carry organic winter squash; other sources are natural food stores, farmers' markets, and food cooperatives.

Strawberries

The FDA pesticide monitoring program reports that 62.8 percent of domestic and 63.8 percent of imported strawberries have pesticide residues. This makes strawberries one of the most contaminated of fruits. The Total Diet Study found evidence of malathion and endosulfan (can cause nervous system damage), iprodione (likely carcinogen), captan (probable carcinogen), and the industrial contaminants and carcinogens, benzene and styrene.

Processed Products. Strawberry jelly and jam can be expected to have the same pesticide residues as the strawberries from which they are made.

Safety Hints. Choose berries that are brightly colored, firm, and with the hulls (caps) still attached. Store them in the refrigerator loosely covered with plastic or a paper towel. Do not hull them until you plan to use them, because hulling causes them to lose vitamin C very quickly. Use the berries within one to two days of purchase. Before using strawberries, hull them and wash with water. Unfortunately, pesticide residues may penetrate the fruit and cannot be removed. To further minimize your exposure to pesticide residues, buy organic strawberries and strawberry products, which may be available at some supermarkets, but more likely at farmers' markets, food cooperatives, and natural food stores.

Sweet Potatoes

Nineteen percent of domestic and 0 percent of imported sweet potatoes had pesticide residues, according to the FDA's pesticide monitoring program. Traces of chlorpropham (may cause tumors), permethrin (possible carcinogen), and dicloran (reported to be relatively safe) were found in the Total Diet Study.

Safety Hints. When shopping for sweet potatoes, look for firm potatoes that have smooth, uniformly colored skins that have no signs of mold or decay. This is important, as sweet potatoes are more perishable than white potatoes. Even if you cut away decayed parts of a sweet potato, the remainder of the potato may taste bad.

Store sweet potatoes in a cool, dark place. Do not refrigerate them. Because sweet potatoes don't store well, buy only as many as you plan to use within a few days. Scrub them with water and a vegetable brush before use. Peeling helps remove surface residue, but some pesticides may have penetrated into the flesh, and they cannot be removed. Cooking may reduce the levels of some of these pesticides. To further minimize exposure to pesticides, buy organic sweet potatoes, which may be available at some supermarkets, but more likely at food cooperatives, farmers' markets, and natural food stores.

Tomatoes

According to the FDA pesticide monitoring program, 25 percent of domestic and 30.4 percent of imported tomatoes had pesticide residues. The Total Diet Study listed chlorpropham (can cause tumors), as well as dicofol and endosulfan (may cause birth defects, cancer, nervous system damage) as residues found on tomato samples.

Processed Products. Foods such as tomato ketchup, tomato sauce, stewed tomatoes, and tomato juice typically have the same pesticide residues as are found in the whole tomatoes from which they are made. The Total Diet Study reported that DDE and endosulfan were found in ketchup; endosulfan in tomato sauce; acephate, carbaryl, endosulfan, and methamidophos in stewed, canned tomatoes; and carbaryl and endosulfan in tomato juice. The USDA Pesticide Data Program found that 30 percent of tomato paste samples contained endosulfan.

Safety Hints. Look for tomatoes that have smooth, unblemished skin. If you need to ripen tomatoes, place them stem up in a well-ventilated area at room temperature and out of direct sunlight. Fully ripened tomatoes can be refrigerated for two to three days. Place unwashed tomatoes in a plastic bag that has holes in it and put the bag in the refrigerator crisper. Do not re-refrigerate tomatoes once you have removed them from the refrigerator. Wash tomatoes with water before using. If you have leftover cut tomatoes, refrigerate them within two hours of cutting. Store them in an airtight container or cover them with plastic wrap and refrigerate.

The best way to minimize exposure to pesticides in tomatoes and tomato products is to buy organic. Some supermarkets carry organic tomatoes and tomato products, as do many food cooperatives, farmers' markets, and natural food stores.

Turnips

One hundred percent of domestic turnips were free of pesticides, according to the FDA's pesticide monitoring program. Turnips are treated with pesticides, however, and some of them include chlorpyrifos (can cause nervous system damage), endosulfan (may cause birth defects, cancer, nervous system damage), and permethrin (possible carcinogen).

Safety Hints. Shop for turnips that are round, small to medium in size, with a smooth, firm surface. If the tops are attached, they should be fresh and green. Avoid large turnips. When storing turnips, cut off the greens and place them in a plastic bag and refrigerate. These should keep for several days. Place the turnips in a separate plastic bag and refrigerate as well; they should last up to one week.

Wash turnip greens under running water, cleaning each leaf separately. Wash turnips using water and a vegetable brush. If the turnips have been waxed, use a vegetable peeler to remove a thin layer of skin, because wax seals in pesticide residues. To minimize pesticide exposure, buy organic turnips, which may be available at some supermarkets, but more likely at farmers' markets, natural food stores, and food cooperatives.

Water Chestnuts

According to the FDA's pesticide monitoring program, 14.3 percent of imported water chestnuts had pesticide residues (there were no domestic figures reported). Most of the water chestnuts consumed in the United States are canned.

Safety Hints. If you buy fresh water chestnuts, which are found primarily in Asian food markets, look for sooty, smooth-skinned chestnuts that are very hard and free of soft spots. Store unwashed and unpeeled in a loosely closed paper or plastic bag in the refrigerator crisper, where they should keep for up to two weeks. Before using, wash with water and a vegetable brush, peel, and immediately place them in cold water to prevent discoloration.

To minimize pesticide exposure, you can look for organic water chestnuts. Asian markets will be the most likely place to find these vegetables.

Watermelon

Eighty percent of domestic and 29.4 percent of imported watermelons had pesticide residues, according to the FDA's pesticide monitoring program. The only pesticide residue found on the latest Total Diet Study analyses was methomyl (can cause nervous system damage). Other pesticides used on watermelon include captan, dicofol, fenvalerate, and methyl bromide (see Appendix).

Safety Hints. If you buy an uncut watermelon, look for one that has a relatively smooth surface with a slightly dull rind. The ends of the melon should be rounded and the underside of the melon should have a creamy color. If you buy a cut melon, look for firm, juicy pulp that is free from white streaks. The seeds should be black or dark brown in regular melons and small and white in seedless varieties. Avoid watermelons that have pale pulp or white streaks.

Before eating an uncut watermelon, scrub the rind with a vegetable brush and water, or use a diluted chlorine bleach solution: one teaspoon of bleach in one gallon of water. Rinse the melon thoroughly before cutting. To reduce your exposure to pesticide residues, buy organic watermelons, which may be available at some supermarkets but more likely at food cooperatives, natural food stores, and farmers' markets.

CHAPTER 9

Grains and Grain Products

Grains and grain products—breads, cereals, pasta—are the most abundant foods in the world. Technically, grains are defined as the seed-bearing fruits of grasses and include wheat, oats, rye, rice, barley, and many others. Amaranth, buckwheat, and quinoa are actually fruits, but they are usually included in the grain category because they look like, and we treat them like, grains.

Grains are low in fat, high in fiber, and provide many vitamins and minerals. Whole grains are more nutritious than refined grains, because processed grains have had their nutritious layers—the bran and germ—removed. Some nutrients are added back to refined grains, but often not all those that were removed. Therefore, whole grains and whole-grain products are your best nutritional bet.

In this chapter we will discuss how you can help ensure that you and your family consume the safest forms of grains and grain products.

PESTICIDES AND GRAINS

Grains and grain products are a mixed bag when it comes to pesticide residues. The FDA pesticide monitoring program found that among domestic grains overall,

41.6 percent had pesticide residues. The breakdown was as follows:

Table 4
Percentage of Grains and Grain Products with Pesticide Residues

	Domestic	Imported
Wheat & wheat products	53.2	15
Oats & oat products	22.2	25
Barley & barley products	8.1	0
Rice & rice products	34.1	11.1

Pesticides contaminate grains in three ways: when they are applied to growing crops, when pesticide residues are left behind in the environment, and when pesticides are applied to stored grains. Although the first two ways do contribute some residues, the most likely source of pesticide residues is the treatment of grains after harvest.

Among the pesticides applied to grains are organophosphates such as malathion and chlorpyrifos, which can cause nervous system damage, and the pyrethroids such as permethrin and deltamethrin, which are probable carcinogens. Pesticides from both categories are typically used together for maximum protection of the grains. When conventionally grown grains are stored, fungicides are applied to prevent mold and insecticides are used to ward off hungry insects. These are applied in a gaseous form called fumigants. Over time, the pesticides applied to stored grains gradually break down so that the amount left on the grain is significantly less than what was applied, although some does remain. You can significantly reduce your exposure to pesticide residues from grains if you purchase organically grown grains or items made from organic crops.

AFLATOXINS

Aflatoxins are toxins that are produced by a mold that can grow in grains, legumes, seeds, and nuts. The FDA has determined that aflatoxins can cause cancer in animals and they can cause liver damage as well, but the agency allows low levels of these contaminants to be present in foods because it considers their presence to be "unavoidable." Its position is that occasional ingestion of small amounts of the toxins present little risk to human life.

To make sure foods don't contain what the FDA considers to be unsafe levels, the USDA's Grain Inspection, Packers and Stockyards Administration (GIPSA) tests foods susceptible to the mold, including corn, wheat, soybeans, rice, popcorn, corn meal, and corn gluten meal. Peanuts, peanut butter, and nuts that grow on trees (e.g., pecans, almonds, walnuts) are also analyzed (see chapter 9).

SAFETY GUIDELINES FOR GRAINS AND GRAIN PRODUCTS

Grains are not only low in fat, free of cholesterol, and great sources of complex carbohydrates, fiber, protein, iron, magnesium, and many of the B vitamins, they are also relatively easy to store and use. Here are some general guidelines to consider when buying and storing grains and grain products:

- If you buy packaged grain products, check for a "sell by" date on the package. You shouldn't buy more than you think you will use by the date unless you plan to refrigerate or freeze the product.

- The three enemies of grains are light, air, and moisture. Therefore, store grain flours, meal, flakes (e.g., oats, rye), grits, and groats (the product of crushed hulled grains such as barley and oats) in airtight containers and keep in a cool, dark place. You can refrigerate or freeze grains as well, which helps extend their shelf life and prevent insect infestation and mold.

- Check grain items frequently for signs of mold. If you find mold on whole grains, flour, or other grain products, throw away the item immediately. Most mycotoxins (toxins produced by molds; alfatoxin is one) do not break down and are not destroyed by cooking, so you cannot safely salvage moldy grain foods.

SPECIFIC GRAINS AND GRAIN PRODUCTS

Amaranth

Amaranth is technically an edible seed, not a grain, that is grown primarily in South America, but with limited crops in the United States. The FDA pesticide monitoring program reported that 50 percent of domestic and only 4 percent of imported edible seeds sampled had pesticide residues.

Processed Products. Amaranth flour is used to make breads, crackers, and other baked goods. It can be expected to have the same pesticides as the amaranth from which it is made.

Safety Hints. Amaranth is one of the richest sources of protein in the plant family. It can be purchased in packages or in bulk at natural food stores, food cooperatives, or farmers' markets, which typically carry organically grown amaranth. Store amaranth in an airtight container and place it in the refrigerator, where it should keep for up to one year.

Barley

Barley is an often overlooked grain that is high in protein (one cup of cooked barley has the same amount of protein as one cup of milk) and is also a very good source of niacin, thiamin, and fiber. It also appears to be a safe grain to enjoy. The FDA's pesticide monitoring program found that 8.1 percent of domestic and 0 percent of imported barley and barley products had pesticide residues. Pesticides approved for use on barley include 2, 4-D (may cause birth defects); disulfoton, piperonyl butoxide, and parathion (can cause nervous system damage); endosulfan (may cause birth defects, cancer, nervous system damage); mancozeb (probable carcinogen); methyl bromide (see Appendix); and pyrethrins (likely carcinogens).

Processed Products. Barley comes in several varieties that vary in color, texture, and flavor, and include hulled whole-grain barley, pearl barley (the most common), scotch barley (darker in color), hull-less barley (dark brown), and barley flakes (can be used like oatmeal). As reported, pesticide contamination is very low.

Safety Hints. Barley should be stored in an airtight container and kept in a cool, dark place. It can be refrigerated or frozen to extend its shelf life, which is at least six months unrefrigerated. To minimize your exposure to pesticide residues, look for organic barley, most often available in natural food stores, farmers' markets, and food cooperatives.

Bread and Bread Products

Breads and bread products (e.g., rolls, English muffins, bagels) can be made from many different grains, and in some cases a mixture of grains, which means these products will contain the same pesticide residues as the grains from which they were made. See individual grains in this section for a list of the pesticides typically associated with them.

Safety Hints. Select bread, rolls, or bagels made with organic whole grains. These products provide more nutrients and fiber than conventionally produced products, and you are spared pesticide residues and additives. One additive you especially want to avoid is potassium bromate (see chapter 4), which causes cancer in laboratory animals.

Bulgur

Bulgur is the kernels of whole wheat that have been boiled, dried, and cracked. It is similar to cracked wheat, except it has been precooked. Because it is a wheat product, it has been exposed to the same pesticides as wheat. According to the FDA pesticide monitoring program, 52.3 percent of domestic and 15 percent of imported wheat and wheat products showed traces of pesticide residues.

Hundreds of pesticides are approved for use on wheat crops, and some of them include atrazine (linked with cancer); benomyl (to be withdrawn by 2005); endosulfan (may cause birth defects, cancer, nervous system damage); carbaryl, chlorpyrifos, disulfoton, malathion, and phorate (can cause nervous system damage); diuron (known carcinogen); mancozeb (probable carcinogen); and pyrethrins and thiabendazole (likely carcinogens).

Safety Hints. Bulgur can be found in supermarkets, often near the rice, pasta, or specialty foods, and is often labeled as "tabbouleh." It is a common product in the bulk foods sections of natural food stores, where you are also more likely to find organic bulgur. Bulgur should be stored in airtight containers in a cool, dry place. It will keep in the refrigerator or at room temperature for five to six months or in the freezer indefinitely. To prepare bulgur, do not rinse it before cooking. Bulgur cooks quickly (about fifteen minutes) and more than doubles in volume during the process, so make sure you put it in a large enough pot. Typically, you need to add three cups of boiling water to one cup of dry bulgur. Prepared bulgur can be refrigerated or frozen if kept in airtight containers for later use.

Cereals

Cereals are a popular food in the United States, especially among children, so it's important for you to know what's in your cereal bowl. The pesticide residues in any cereal will depend on the grain(s) from which it was made, so look at the individual entries for corn, wheat, oats, and so on for possible contaminants.

In addition, however, most commercial brands of cereal also have many additives, including sugar, artificial colors, artificial flavors, and preservatives that add no nutritional value to the cereal and can in fact be detrimental. Most cereals contain BHT, an additive that is "reasonably anticipated to be a human carcinogen" (see chapter 4).

Safety Hints. To avoid pesticides, added sugars, and artificial ingredients, especially BHT, choose organic cereals. Most supermarkets carry organic brands, but you can also find them in natural food stores and food cooperatives.

Corn

Fifty percent of domestic and 0 percent of imported corn and corn products showed evidence of pesticide contamination, according to the FDA's pesticide monitoring program. In chapter 7, we looked at sweet corn and its use as a vegetable, both fresh and canned, but here we consider products made from corn, such as corn meal and corn grits, which are made from field corn; popcorn; corn chips; and corn-based cereals.

Corn is treated with a variety of pesticides, including alachlor (known carcinogen) and diuron, captan and mancozeb (probable carcinogens), methyl bromide (see Appendix), and disulfoton (can cause nervous system damage), among others. Another concern is that field corn may be contaminated with aflatoxin, a naturally occurring mold that is known to cause cancer in laboratory animals (see "Aflatoxins" in this chapter).

Processed Products. In samples of popcorn popped with oil analyzed in the Total Diet Study, researchers found evidence of the industrial contaminants benzene and styrene (carcinogens) as well as tetrachloroethylene (probable carcinogen), toluene, and xylene; the pesticides methoxychlor (can alter hormone function); malathion and pirimiphos-methyl (can cause nervous system damage); and PCBs. The study found no residues in corn grits, but did find methoxychlor in corn flakes, and industrial contaminants tetrachloroethylene, benzene and styrene (both carcinogens), chloroform (probable carcinogen), toluene, and xylene in corn chips.

Because 40 percent of the US corn crop is genetically modified, there's a good chance these corn products, as well as others that contain corn in the form of corn syrup, corn meal, corn starch, and corn oil, contain modified corn. See chapter 5 for more on genetically modified foods.

Safety Hints. To minimize your exposure to pesticides and genetically modified corn and corn products, you can choose organic products. Many supermarkets carry some organic foods in either a natural foods section or interspersed with conventional items (e.g., organic corn flakes will appear alongside conventional corn flake products). Natural food stores, food cooperatives, and farmers' markets are other sources for organic corn products. See the Appendix for names of some suppliers.

A bonus when you buy organic corn products is that you avoid exposure to genetically modified corn. Look for products that say "non-GMO corn."

Couscous

This grain is made from the semolina of durum wheat, which is native to North Africa. Couscous has long been imported into the United States, but it has also been made here since 1993. Because it is a wheat product, it is treated with the same pesticides as whole wheat. According to the FDA pesticide monitoring program, 52.3 percent of domestic and 15 percent of imported wheat and wheat products showed traces of pesticide residues.

Hundreds of pesticides are approved for use on wheat crops, and some of them include atrazine (linked with cancer); benomyl (to be withdrawn by 2005); endosulfan (may cause birth defects, cancer, nervous system damage); carbaryl, chlorpyrifos, disulfoton, malathion, and phorate (can cause nervous system damage); diuron (known carcinogen); mancozeb (probable carcinogen); and pyrethrins and thiabendazole (likely carcinogens).

Safety Hints. Couscous can be found in supermarkets, often in the same aisles as rice and pasta, or in a specialty section. Several companies have boxed couscous and offer both plain and flavored varieties. It is also available in bulk bin sections in natural food stores.

To store uncooked couscous, place it in an airtight container at room temperature, refrigerated, or frozen. Because it is a precooked product, it can be prepared in less than ten minutes by just adding boiling water and letting it sit. Prepared couscous can be refrigerated or frozen.

Oats

Analysis by the FDA's pesticide monitoring program revealed that 22.2 percent of domestic and 25 percent of imported oats and oat products had pesticide residues. Some of the pesticides applied to oats include endosulfan (may cause cancer, birth defects, nervous system damage), diuron (known carcinogen), malathion (can cause nervous system damage), mancozeb (probable carcinogen), methyl bromide (see Appendix), and pyrethrins (likely carcinogens).

Processed Products. The Total Diet Study found evidence of clopyralid (an herbicide that causes reproductive problems in animals) in the samples of oat ring cereal it inspected. No reports were available for other oat items, such as oatmeal, oat flour, or oat breads. However, these products can be expected to contain the same pesticides as the oats from which they were made.

Safety Hints. Store oats in an airtight container and keep in a cool place. If unrefrigerated, oats should keep for about six months; refrigerated or frozen, they will keep one year. You can minimize your exposure to pesticides by purchasing organic oats, which may be available at natural food stores, farmers markets, and food cooperatives.

Pasta

The most popular pasta in the United States is made from semolina, which is coarsely ground durum wheat. Therefore, pasta made from wheat can be expected to have the same pesticides as the wheat from which it was made. Samples of macaroni analyzed in the Total Diet Study found residues of chlorpyrifos and malathion, while samples of egg noodles revealed the same pesticides, as well as endosulfan (may cause birth defects, cancer, nervous system damage) and diazinon.

Pastas are also made from other grains, such as amaranth, corn, and rice. These products can be expected to contain the same pesticides as the grains from which they were made.

Safety Hints. Levels of microbes can be very high in dried pasta; therefore, never chew on or eat uncooked pasta. Boiling pasta kills most microorganisms. Fresh pasta, however, may pose a problem, because it can harbor bacteria. Unless you are confident that the fresh pasta you plan to eat has been prepared under sanitary conditions (remember that about 50 percent of the general population has the microorganism *Staphylococcus aureus*—which can cause food poisoning—on their hands), it is best to avoid it. If you make your own fresh pasta, make sure you thoroughly wash your hands and all the preparation surfaces before making the pasta. Fresh pasta should also be refrigerated until you are ready to cook it.

To help avoid exposure to pesticides in any type of pasta, you should look for organic varieties, which can be found in some supermarkets, as well as natural food stores and food cooperatives.

Rice

According to the FDA pesticide monitoring program, 34.1 percent of domestic and 11.1 percent of imported rice and rice products had detectable pesticide residues. The USDA Pesticide Data Program identified malathion in 11 percent of rice samples and piperonyl butoxide (possible carcinogen) in 18 percent. Other pesticides applied to rice include carbaryl (can cause nervous system damage), iprodione and thiabendazole (likely carcinogens), and methyl bromide (see Appendix).

Processed Products. The Total Diet Study found traces of the herbicide quinclorac in white rice, crisp rice cereal, and rice cereal for infants. The EPA has stated that it is reasonably certain quinclorac is not harmful and that it is not a carcinogen. There are more than 7,000 varieties of rice, but the most common ones seen in the United States number less than a dozen. Brown rice is more nutritious than white rice, which has had its germ and bran layer removed. Types of rice you may see on the shelves include arborio rice (an Italian-grown rice), basmati (often seen in Middle Eastern markets), long-grain white rice, instant or quick white rice (dehydrated rice), jasmine, mochi, wild pecan rice (brown), and wild rice (which is really a grass but usually put in the rice category).

Safety Hints. Rice should be stored in an airtight container and left in a cool, dark place. Unrefrigerated rice should keep for about one year, but you can extend its shelf life by refrigerating or freezing it. Cooked rice can be kept frozen for up to six months.

To minimize your exposure to pesticides, buy organic rice, which may be available at farmers' markets, food cooperatives, and natural food stores.

Rye

The FDA's pesticide monitoring program does not report specifically on levels of contaminants in rye; however, grains in general are considered to be safe foods. Some of the pesticides used to treat rye include atrazine (linked to prostate cancer), benomyl (to be withdrawn by 2005), diuron (known carcinogen), endosulfan (may cause birth defects, cancer, nervous system damage), malathion (can cause nervous system damage), mancozeb (probable carcinogen), methyl bromide (see Appendix), and pyrethrins (likely carcinogens).

Processed Products. The Total Diet Study found evidence of chlorpyrifos, malathion, pirimiphos methyl, and diphenyl 2-ethylhexyl phosphate (all can cause nervous system damage) in samples of rye bread. Rye flour can be expected to have the same pesticide residues as the rye from which it is made.

Safety Hints. Overall, rye products offer more health benefits than risks. To further minimize your exposure to pesticides, buy organically grown whole rye products. Whole rye, unlike processed rye, is more nutritious because it includes the fiber-rich bran. Whole rye products may be available in some supermarkets, but more likely in natural food stores, farmers' markets, and food cooperatives.

Wheat

According to the FDA's pesticide monitoring program, 53.2 percent of domestic and 15 percent of imported wheat and wheat products contained pesticide residues. Hundreds of pesticides are approved for use on wheat crops, and some of them include atrazine (linked with cancer); benomyl (to be withdrawn by 2005); endosulfan (may cause birth defects, cancer, nervous system damage); carbaryl, chlorpyrifos, disulfoton, malathion, and phorate (can cause nervous system damage); diuron (known carcinogen); mancozeb (probable carcinogen); and pyrethrins and thiabendazole (likely carcinogens).

Processed Products. The Total Diet Study found a variety of contaminants in wheat products, which we list here:

- Bagel (plain): chlorpyrifos and malathion.
- Cracked wheat bread: 2,4-D, chlorpyrifos, malathion, and diphenyl 2-ethylhexyl phosphate.
- English muffins (plain): chlorpyrifos and malathion.
- Flour tortillas: chlorpyrifos, malathion, and diphenyl 2-ethylhexyl phosphate (all can cause nervous system damage).
- Pretzels: chlorpyrifos and malathion.
- Saltine crackers: chlorpyrifos and malathion.
- Shredded wheat cereal: chlorpyrifos and malathion.
- White bread: industrial contaminants benzene and styrene (both carcinogens), as well as chloroform (possible carcinogen), and toluene. Also pesticides chlorpyrifos, malathion, diphenyl 2-ethylhexyl phosphate, and iprodione (likely carcinogen).
- Whole wheat bread: chlorpyrifos and malathion.

Safety Hints. To minimize exposure to pesticides, buy organic wheat products. Many supermarkets now carry these items, either in a natural foods section or interspersed with conventional foods (e.g., organic pretzels next to the conventional pretzels in the snack aisle). Natural food stores, farmers' markets, and food cooperatives also carry these products. See the Appendix for a list of some suppliers.

CHAPTER 10

Legumes and Nuts

Legumes (beans and peas) and nuts are all-important plant sources of protein and have been staples of the diets of many cultures around the world for millennia. They are cholesterol-free, low in sodium, and good sources of iron, magnesium, fiber, and potassium, in addition to protein. However, it's pretty safe to say that your great-great-grandparents and those who came before them didn't have to worry about most of the contaminants that can be found in many of the bean, pea, and nut crops of today.

You and your family can enjoy all the different types of beans, legumes, and nuts, without worrying about contaminants, if you follow a few guidelines. This chapter tells you all you need to know about making these nutritious foods a healthy part of your diet.

Here are the safety guidelines for legumes and nuts:

- After purchasing dry beans or peas, sort and clean them carefully, as debris such as tiny stones frequently can be found in them. You can spread the beans or peas out on a light-colored towel or baking sheet to help you better see any foreign objects.
- Beans, peas, and nuts are best stored in airtight containers and kept at 70° F or lower, as higher temperatures cause their quality to decline faster. Keeping

them in the refrigerator or freezer is a good choice
as well.

• Dry beans and peas should be used within twelve
  months of purchase.
• Frozen cooked beans should be used within six
  months.
• Use refrigerated cooked beans within four to five
  days.
• To repel insects, place a dried hot pepper in the
  container holding your beans or peas.
• When cooking dry beans, do not add salt to the
  water until just before they are done. Adding it
  sooner will cause the beans to become tough.

LET'S GO SHOPPING

Dry Beans

In the Total Diet Study, two types of dry beans were
prepared and analyzed. Boiled pinto beans showed traces
of iprodione (likely carcinogen), while cooked kidney
beans showed no pesticide residues. Some of the pesticides applied to dry beans (e.g., pinto, kidney, black,
navy) include captan and thiabendazole (likely carcinogens), carboxin and dicofol (may cause birth defects, cancer, nervous system damage), and aldicarb, dimethoate,
and methyl parathion (can cause nervous system
damage).

A rare but serious type of food poisoning associated
with kidney beans is red kidney bean poisoning. The
toxin, phytohaemagglutinin, is found in many species of
beans, but it is highest in red kidneys. Poisoning is caused
by eating raw or even undercooked kidney beans, which
can occur in slow cookers that do not reach an internal
temperature high enough to destroy the toxin (165° F).
Symptoms (severe nausea, vomiting, diarrhea) come on
rapidly and resolve within hours.

Processed Products. In the Total Diet Study, samples of canned pork and beans showed residues of 2-chloroethyl linoleate, 2-chloroethyl myristate, and 2-chloroethyl palmitate, as well as chlorpyrifos, all of which can cause nervous system damage. Other processed bean products include various varieties of canned beans, refried beans, chili with beans, and bean dips. These products can be expected to contain the same pesticide residues as the beans from which they were made.

Safety Hints. Dry beans can be purchased in packages or in bulk. In either case, store and clean beans as suggested in the guidelines. To prepare beans, rinse them in a colander or strainer. If you soak the beans overnight before cooking them, discard the soaking water and use fresh water in which to cook the beans. When cooking any beans, but especially red kidney beans, make sure they are thoroughly cooked to prevent red kidney bean poisoning.

Although cooking may reduce pesticide residues, you can minimize your risk even further by using organic beans, which are available in some supermarkets as well as natural food stores, food cooperatives, and farmers' markets. See the Appendix for a list of some suppliers.

Lentils

No specific reports on pesticide residues are available from the FDA or the Total Diet Study. Some of the pesticides approved for use on lentil crops include carbaryl, dimethoate, malathion, and methomyl (all can cause nervous system damage), and thiabendazole (likely carcinogen).

Safety Hints. Lentils are a legume and a rich source of protein, B vitamins, and fiber, and overall considered to be a safe addition to your diet. Lentils can be purchased in packages (usually one pound) or in bulk, and may be brown or red. If you buy lentils in bulk, examine them carefully for tiny marks or holes, which may indicate insect damage, and for tiny stones. Store and clean lentils as suggested in the guidelines. Lentils can be kept for up to one year in an airtight container.

Before cooking lentils, rinse them under cold water in a strainer or colander. Once cooked, lentils should be stored in a covered container in the refrigerator, where they should keep for three to four days. You can also freeze cooked lentils for up to six months.

To minimize exposure to pesticide residues, buy organic lentils, which may be available at farmers' markets, food cooperatives, and natural food stores.

Mixed Nuts

The Total Diet Study analyzed mixed nuts (without peanuts) and reported finding residues of lindane (probable carcinogen), as well as the industrial contaminants benzene and styrene (carcinogens), tetrachloroethylene (probable carcinogen), toluene, and xylene. Below is some information on different nuts.

Almonds. One hundred percent of the domestic almonds and almond products analyzed by the FDA's pesticide monitoring program were free of pesticide residues. No figures for imported almonds were given. Some of the pesticides used on almonds include benomyl (to be withdrawn by 2005), captan (probable carcinogen), endosulfan (may cause birth defects, cancer, nervous system damage), iprodione and pyrethrins (likely carcinogens), and carbaryl, chlorpyrifos, diazinon, malathion, and parathion (all can cause nervous system damage). Almonds are also susceptible to contamination by aflatoxin, a mold that develops on some nuts and which causes cancer in laboratory animals.

When possible, choose raw, organic almonds or almond butter, available at food cooperatives, natural food stores, and farmers' markets; also see the Appendix. Store almonds in an airtight container in the refrigerator, where they should keep for up to six months. Discard almonds that have dark spots or mold or that taste bad.

Cashews. In the FDA's pesticide monitoring program, 22.2 percent of the imported cashews analyzed showed pesticide residues. No figures were available for domestic cashews. Pesticides used to treat cashews include aluminum phosphide, methyl bromide (see Glossary), and phosphine. Cashews are also susceptible to contamination by aflatoxin, a mold that can cause cancer in laboratory animals (see chapter 9).

To reduce your exposure to pesticide residues, buy organic cashews or cashew butter, which are available at some natural food stores, food cooperatives, or farmers' markets; also see the Appendix. Store cashews in an airtight container in the refrigerator, where they should keep for up to six months. Throw away any cashews that have dark spots or mold or that taste bad.

Pecans. No specific information on residues for pecans is available. However, the FDA's pesticide monitoring program found that 0 percent of domestic and 11.1 percent of imported "other nuts" had pesticide residues. Some of the pesticides used on pecans include carbaryl, dicofol, dimethoate, endosulfan, lindane, malathion, methyl bromide, parathion, and ziram. Pecans are also susceptible to contamination by aflatoxin, a mold that causes cancer in laboratory animals (see chapter 9).

To reduce your exposure to pesticide residues, buy organic pecans, which can be found in some natural food stores, food cooperatives, or farmers' markets; also see the Appendix. Store pecans in an airtight container in the refrigerator, where they should keep for up to six months. Discard any pecans that develop mold or dark spots or that taste bad.

Peanuts

The FDA's pesticide monitoring program found pesticide residues in 22.2 percent of domestic and 50 percent of imported peanuts and peanut products. Samples of dry roasted peanuts analyzed in the Total Diet Study revealed residues of DDE, endosulfan, toxaphene, and dieldrin (all may cause birth defects, cancer, nervous system damage), and chlorpyrifos (can cause nervous system damage). Peanuts may also be contaminated with aflatoxin, a naturally occurring mold that causes cancer in laboratory animals (see chapter 9).

Processed Products. Peanut butter and peanut oil can be expected to have the same residues as the peanuts from which they are made. In fact, the Total Diet Study found evidence of the industrial contaminants benzene and styrene (carcinogens), chloroform (probable carcinogen), toluene, and xylene in peanut butter, along with DDE, dieldrin, toxaphene, endosulfan, and chlorpyrifos in peanut butter samples.

Safety Hints. Peanuts present greater health risks than many other nuts. It is best to buy organically raised peanuts, preferably in the shell. Store them in an airtight container in the refrigerator, where they should keep for several months. Throw away any peanuts that have mold or dark spots, or that taste bad. Organic peanut butter and peanut oil are also available, often in natural food stores, food cooperatives, or farmers' markets; also see the Appendix.

Soybeans

Soybeans are the second most planted and harvested crop in the United States. Many people don't realize that soybeans and soybean products (e.g., flour, meal, grits, oil) are in many foods, from soups to cereals to canned pasta. Thus it's not only people who eat tofu and soyburgers who should be aware of how soybean crops are treated.

Some of the pesticides applied to soybeans include alachlor (likely carcinogen); captan and thiodicarb (probable carcinogens); acephate, carbaryl, dimethoate, malathion, and phorate (all can cause nervous system damage); and methyl bromide (see Glossary).

Genetically Engineered? In 2003, 81 percent of the soybeans grown in the United States were genetically modified. At the same time, there were about 14 million acres of non-GE soybeans in the United States. The demand for nonmodified soybeans is growing, and farmers are now being paid a premium to produce them. As the number of non-GE soybean acres increases, so will the number of products that will contain nonengineered soybeans, although there are many nonengineered products from which to choose now.

Processed Products. The number and variety of processed soybean products are growing steadily, and there is an increasing demand for non-GE soybean products as well. Soybean-based "meats," "cheeses," milk, frozen desserts, and snacks, along with tofu, soy flour, soy sauce, and soybean oil, are considered mainstream items in many supermarkets. Among the brands of soybean-based products are Eden Foods, Lightlife, Yves, Morningstar, Boca, Loma Linda, Veggie Patch, Galaxy, Soy Delicious, and others (see Appendix).

Safety Hints. When buying soy products, look for those that say "no GMO soybeans" or "organic" on the label. Such products are available in many supermarkets, but you'll also find them in natural food stores and food cooperatives.

Split Peas

Split peas are either green or yellow. Some of the pesticides applied to split peas are ethalfluralin (causes cancer in lab animals) and fenvalerate and methyl parathion (can cause nervous system damage).

Safety Hints. Store and clean split peas as suggested in the guidelines for legumes and nuts. Before cooking them, rinse them thoroughly in a colander with water. When you add split peas to cooking water, the good ones will sink and the bad ones will float to the top for easy removal. To minimize exposure to pesticides, buy organically grown split peas. These can most often be found in natural food stores, farmers' markets, and food cooperatives.

CHAPTER 11

Meat

Hardly a week goes by that we don't hear a news report or study results about a problem with the meat supply in the United States or abroad. Sometimes it's a recall of ground beef because of contamination with E. coli, which happens dozens of times each year; another time it may be a series of stories about mad cow disease, as when a cow with the disease was discovered in Washington state in December 2003; or it may be a study telling how meat consumption has been linked with colon cancer. Along with these and other stories come the claims by both sides of the issues: from the ranchers, beef producers, and government agencies who keep insisting the meat supply is safe, to the consumer advocate groups and medical professionals who urge caution or even avoidance of meat products.

Any way you slice it, meat and meat consumption are a health issue in America. That's why in this chapter we look at some of the important safety factors you need to consider if you and your family eat meat and meat products.

MEAT AND CONTAMINANTS

Some of the information about meat you rarely hear concerns problems like the fact that nearly all the meat in the United States contains residues of toxic chemicals. According to the Humane Farming Association, only a small percentage of meat processed in US slaughterhouses is ever tested for drug and chemical residues. That means the vast majority of meat enters the market untested for these contaminants.

These chemicals are used primarily for two reasons: to promote growth (and thus increase profits) or to prevent disease or infestation from parasites and other disease-causing agents. Toxins can also enter the meat supply unintentionally, as when cattle eat grass or drink water that has been contaminated with dioxins, PBCs, or other industrial contaminants. In fact, the Environmental Protection Agency (EPA) reports that most of the dioxin you are exposed to comes from eating red meat, dairy products, and fish, which means these animals are ingesting the toxins from the environment and passing them along to you.

In the case of feed, about 80 percent of the pesticides used in the United States are applied to the four crops that are fed to livestock: corn, wheat, cotton, and soybean. Because these crops are not for direct human consumption, there are no limits on the amounts of pesticides that can be used. These heavily treated crops are then fed to beef cattle, dairy cattle, hogs, and sheep, and the toxins accumulate in their bodies, which means you are ultimately exposed to the pesticides in the meat you eat.

Pesticides and other toxins are also applied to the exterior of livestock to ward off flies and parasites. In addition, about 50 percent of the beef cattle in the United States have a steroid (hormone) implant in their ear, which sends the drug directly into the animal to stimulate growth. These hormones are then present in the meat you eat.

MEAT AND FOODBORNE DISEASE

In April 2001, 14.5 million pounds of ready-to-eat meat and poultry products—luncheon meat, ham, sausage, hot dogs, and corn dogs—were recalled by the Bar-S Foods Company because of possible contamination with *Listeria monocytogenes*. Listeriosis, the foodborne illness that is caused by *listeria*, can be especially serious, even fatal, to infants, the elderly, pregnant women, and people who have a chronic or immune system disease. One feature of listeriosis is that once people eat food that has been contaminated with the microorganisms, it can take up to three weeks for them to become ill. Generally, individuals who are healthy are only mildly affected by the illness, if at all.

When it comes to meat and foodborne illnesses, there are some things you should keep in mind. First, meat is one of the primary sources of foodborne disease in the United States. That means you need to be especially careful when you buy, store, and prepare meat and meat products to avoid contamination and to thoroughly destroy disease-causing organisms in them. Second, there are dozens of recalls of meat and meat products each year in the United States, and in many cases, most of the meat is never recovered. That means some people who purchase potentially contaminated meat may consume it and get ill without ever knowing why. (Remember, the CDC estimates that 76 million cases of food poisoning occur in the United States each year, with about 325,000 hospitalizations and more than 5,000 deaths.)

Meat Recalls

Recalls of meat and poultry by manufacturers because of known or possible contamination are not unusual, and in fact occur more often than once per week. In 2000, for example, there were 76 cases of meat and poultry recalls. In one case, Omaha Steaks recalled 22,000 pounds of ground beef because of possible contamination with E. coli, but only 10 pounds were ever recovered. How many people ate the remaining 21,990 pounds? In the same year, Moyer Packing recalled 346,700 pounds of meat, and recovered only 3,409 pounds, less than 10 percent.

These two examples are by no means unusual; in fact, between 1995 and 2000, a total of 275 recalls were made for meat products. The recalled meat totaled more than 140 million pounds, yet less than 30 percent of it was ever recovered. Nearly two-thirds of the ground beef recalled during that time span was never recovered, and 91 percent of the recalled ground beef was being called back because of deadly E. coli contamination.

NATURAL, ORGANIC, FREE-RANGE: WHAT DOES IT MEAN?

If you have concerns about the hormones, antibiotics, pesticides, and other contaminants in conventionally raised meat products, if mad cow disease worries are lurking in the back of your mind, and if you're not ready to kick the meat habit, you may want to consider "cleaner" meat. Perhaps you've gone to a natural food store and looked at the selections in the "natural," "free-range," or "organic" meat counter. What do these labels mean?

Free-range cows, pigs, and sheep, according to the USDA, are those livestock that must be fed grass and allowed to live outdoors. However, these guidelines are not only vague (e.g., there are no criteria as to the size of the area for the animals or the amount of space for each one; also, the grass they eat can be treated with fertilizers and pesticides), they are rarely verified. In fact, the USDA depends on the word of the farmers themselves that their animals are grass-fed and living on a range.

Natural meats come from animals that were not given hormones or antibiotics. However, they can be fed grains and other feed that has been treated with pesticides.

Certified organic meats come from animals that are not treated with hormones or antibiotics. According to USDA regulations for national organic standards, adopted in 2002, organically raised livestock must also be fed 100 percent organic feed (e.g., no pesticides, sewage sludge, or synthetic fertilizers used), and the meat must be free from irradiation and genetic modification (e.g., the feed cannot contain genetically modified grains). Certified organic meats are rigorously inspected and carry a USDA organic symbol. You can expect to pay more for organic meat, but you won't be getting potentially dangerous contaminants.

The integrity of certified organic meats appears to be in jeopardy, however. In February 2003, Congress passed an appropriations bill that had hundreds of special riders, and one of them allows farmers to feed conventional feed (treated with pesticides) to livestock that is being raised organically if organic feed is more than twice the cost of conventional feed. These farmers' can still legally label their meat "certified organic," even though the livestock are fed contaminated feed. This obscure rider not only undermines the integrity of the organic meat industry, it also allows organic meat producers to commit fraud against unwitting consumers who buy certified organic meat products. As a consumer, you have no way of knowing whether the certified organic meat you buy is *really* organic unless you contact each supplier and ask whether conventional feed is given to their livestock.

GENERAL SAFETY GUIDELINES FOR MEAT

The safest thing for you and your family to do is to eliminate meat from your diet. However, if you aren't ready to make that change, there are other steps you can take to minimize your risk of exposure to pesticides, food poisoning, and drugs associated with the meat you eat:

- Buy meat that has been organically produced. Organic meats are usually available at natural food markets and food cooperatives. To find a supplier near you, you can visit the Web site for the Organic Consumers group, www.organicconsumers.org/pure-link.html You may want to contact the supplier to see if the livestock are fed conventional feed.

- Each week, replace several meat-based meals with other nutritious choices, such as lentils, beans, soy-based foods (tofu, tempeh), pasta, vegetables, and grains. The American Dietetic Association has stated that a plant-based diet is a healthy choice and can fully meet the needs of all Americans, from children to the elderly, "and provide healthy benefits in the prevention and treatment of certain diseases." You can get more information about the health benefits of a plant-based diet and ideas for meatless meals at www.meatout.org/about.html; www.pcrm.org (Physicians Committee for Responsible Medicine); and www.eatright.org/Public/GovernmentAffairs/17084.cfm (American Dietetic Association's position paper on a vegetarian diet).

- Always cook meat thoroughly and check the temperature with a meat thermometer. Do not depend on color to tell you if a piece of meat has been adequately cooked. Some ground meat, for example, may turn brown before the safe temperature of 160° F has been reached, while other portions may remain pink even when that temperature has been surpassed. If you order ground beef in a restaurant, order it well done.

- Thaw frozen meat in the refrigerator. Gradual defrosting for eight or more hours helps maintain quality of the meat. If you need to defrost meat more quickly, you can place it in a sealed plastic bag and immerse the bag in a pot of cold water for about an hour. If you have a microwave, you can use the DEFROST setting if you plan to cook the meat immediately after defrosting it.

- Marinate meat in the refrigerator. Once the meat has been marinated, discard the marinade, because it contains raw juice from the meat and may contain bacteria.

- If you cut meat on a cutting board, use a plastic board, as wood has grooves that can capture bacteria. Do not use the plastic cutting board for cutting foods other than meats or poultry. Clean the cutting board with soap and hot water after each use.
- Always wash your hands with soap and hot water before and after handling raw meat.
- Do not eat the organs (e.g., brains, kidneys, livers, sweetbreads) of livestock, because toxins accumulate in them. Given the threat of mad cow disease, brains in particular should never be on your menu.
- If you are a fan of smoked meats, be aware that they contain substances called polycyclic aromatic hydrocarbons, which are known carcinogens. Although most people don't eat enough smoked foods for them to be very concerned, they should be looked at as part of the bigger picture: How many other contaminated foods are you and your family already eating? You should also note that the hotter the charcoal or wood burns, the more polycyclic aromatic hydrocarbons are produced. One study found that meats cooked with mesquite (popular in many restaurants) had eight times the levels of polycyclic aromatic hydrocarbons than meat cooked with hardwood charcoal.

LET'S GO SHOPPING

Beef

According to the USDA Economic Research Service, Americans are eating less beef. From 1980 to 2000, beef consumption declined 11 percent, from an average of 72 pounds to 64 pounds per person.

Eating beef can be a risky thing to do. More than 90 percent of the beef cattle raised in the United States are housed on factory farms, which are characterized by overcrowding and a high risk of disease. These cattle are contaminated with pesticides in their feed and in their environment, antibiotics to stimulate growth and help prevent disease, and hormones to speed up the growth process. All of these contaminants can remain in the meat you eat and possibly have a negative effect on your health. For some people, the fact that mad cow disease has been discovered in the United States is yet another concern about beef (see below).

Beef Products. The Total Diet Study looked at various cuts of beef and analyzed them for contaminants (not antibiotics, hormones, or drugs, however). Here are the findings:

- Beef chuck roast (baked): industrial contaminants benzene and styrene (carcinogens) and toluene.
- Beef loin steak: the organochlorine dieldrin (can cause nervous system damage) and DDE (possible carcinogen).
- Beef liver (fried): dieldrin and heptachlor (may cause cancer, birth defects, nervous system damage).
- Ground beef (cooked): the industrial contaminants benzene, dichlorobenzene, styrene, toluene, and xylene, as well as DDE and the organochlorines dieldrin and heptachlor.
- Strained beef (for infants): bromodichloromethane (may be carcinogenic), DDE, chloroform, toluene, and xylene.
- Fast-food hamburger (on a bun): chloroform, DDE, DDT, dieldrin, endosulfan, heptachlor, malathion, styrene, toluene, and xylene.

In the USDA Pesticide Data Program, beef fat was examined. Investigators found that 59 percent of samples had residues, with DDE being one of the main findings.

Mad Cow Disease. Mad cow disease was first diagnosed in England in 1986, and it has now been found in more than thirty countries, including the United States. Its appearance in Washington state in December 2003 brought the disease back into the spotlight and made many Americans stop and think twice about the beef they were eating. Should you be worried about mad cow disease?

Mad cow disease appears to be caused by malformed proteins called prions, which cause proteins in the brain to become distorted, causing holes to develop in the brain. Experts know that the incubation period for mad cow disease is two to eight years, which makes it difficult to monitor and prevent transmission of the disease to other cows.

By the end of 2003, more than 130 people around the world (most in England) had contracted a disease related to mad cow disease, called variant Creutzfeldt-Jakob disease (vCJD), apparently by eating infected beef. Symptoms of vCJD are muscle incoordination, impaired memory, vision problems, difficulties with judgment, and depression. As the disease progresses, mental abilities continue to deteriorate until the patient goes into a coma and dies. There are no known treatments or vaccines to prevent this disease. Experts also do not know what the incubation period for vCJD is, and so anyone who has eaten infected beef today may not develop the disease for many years.

The whole process of mad cow disease is believed to begin when cows eat feed that has been contaminated with infected remains from cows and sheep. The practice of feeding cows (which are vegetarians) feed that contains animal byproducts was practiced by many countries but has since been banned both in the United States and abroad in hopes this will prevent further spread of mad cow disease.

Safety Hints. Unlike microorganisms like E. coli or parasites, prions cannot be destroyed by pasteurization, heating, chemical disinfection, or sterilization. Thus ordering your burger well done won't reduce your risk of getting vCJD. You can, however, take other steps, such as eating only certified organic beef, choosing beef that has minimal chance of contamination from nervous tissue (solid muscle cuts), or eliminating beef from your diet and substituting other, healthier protein choices (see "General Safety Guidelines for Meat").

If you choose conventionally produced beef, you should choose the leanest cuts of beef, such as sirloin and round steak, because pesticides accumulate in fat. Remove all visible fat from any cut of beef.

To help prevent foodborne illness, always cook any beef product to the following temperatures and check with a meat thermometer:

- Fresh beef, medium rare: 145° F
- Fresh beef, medium: 160° F
- Fresh beef, well done: 170° F
- Ground beef: 160° F

Lamb

Lamb consumption in the United States is low: just a little more than 1 pound per person per year, or less than 0.6 percent of total US meat consumption. Lamb meat comes from sheep that are less than one year old. The meat can be expected to contain the same pesticides and additives that are in the animals' feed. The Total Diet Study found DDE in pan-cooked lamb chops.

Safety Hints. Lamb is higher in fat than most beef cuts, so if you choose lamb, make sure you cut off all visible fat. To prevent foodborne illness, lamb should always be cooked to the following temperatures and checked with a meat thermometer:

- Medium rare: 145° F
- Medium: 160° F
- Well done: 170° F

To reduce your risk of exposure to pesticides, antibiotics, and hormones, organically raised lamb is available (see Appendix.)

Hot Dogs and Other Ready-to-Eat Meats

The Total Diet Study found that beef franks contained the industrial contaminants benzene and styrene (carcinogens), as well as DDE, chloroform, and tetrachloroethylene (probable carcinogens), toluene, and xylene. Bologna samples had the same contaminants, and salami samples revealed DDE, dieldrin (may cause birth defects, cancer, nervous system damage), styrene, toluene, and xylene.

Safety Hints. To help prevent listeriosis in people at risk for the disease (elderly, people with a compromised immune system or chronic disease, pregnant women), hot dogs, precooked sausages, pepperoni, and luncheon meats should be heated until steaming before they are consumed, or, even better, they should be avoided entirely.

Ready-to-eat meats often contain additives, such as sulfites, which can cause allergic reactions in some people. Nitrates (carcinogens) and nitrites (react with other substances to form cancer-causing substances) are usually found in these foods as well. In addition, ready-to-eat meats are often high in salt and fat (except for low-fat varieties) and overall not a good nutritional choice.

Pork

From 1980 to 2000, American consumption of pork fell slightly, from an average of 52 pounds to 48 pounds per person. The sales pitch proclaiming that pork is "the other white meat" apparently wasn't as convincing as some pork producers may have hoped. If consumers knew some of the health risks associated with pork production, the number of pounds could drop even further.

The factory farm conditions under which the vast ma-

jority of pigs are raised expose them to many contaminants, including antibiotics, hormones, and drugs (see
chapter 4), which are used both to fatten up the hogs
faster and to help fight the diseases that can spread
quickly throughout a farm because of overcrowded conditions. Hogs are also exposed to pesticides in their feed,
and these contaminants can then be found in pork products. Pork can also be contaminated during processing,
storage, and preparation, which means you need to take
precautions to prevent food poisoning once you get pork
products home.

One of the newest drugs being given to hogs is porcine
somatotropin (PST), a hormone that reduces the fat content of pork. Unfortunately, the human health conse-
quences of ingesting this drug are not known. Another
drug of concern is sulfamethazine, which is used to stimulate growth and to control diseases in pigs. The safety of
this drug has never been proven. In fact, the National
Center for Toxicological Research states that sulfamethazine is a carcinogen. Yet more than 70 percent of pork
producers use sulfamethazine, according to the Humane
Farming Association. Illegal levels have been found in
as many as 10 percent of pig carcasses tested, even
though "legal" levels have never been proven safe.

Pork Products. The Total Diet Study analyzes some
of the many pork products on the market for residues of
pesticides and industrial contaminants. The 2001 results
showed residues of DDE in pork chops, pork sausage,
and pork bacon, while the latter item also had traces of
industrial contaminants, including the known carcinogens
benzene and styrene, as well as tetrachloroethylene
(probable carcinogen), toluene, and xylene. Some pork
products, such as cured ham, bacon, and sausage, are
typically treated with nitrates/nitrites, substances you
should avoid (see chapter 4). Nitrites are carcinogens,
and nitrates react with other substances to form cancer-
causing agents. Processed pork, such as some sausages
and pork luncheon meats, may contain sulfites, a
known allergen.

Safety Hints. The safest pork products to eat are those that have been raised organically. In this way you can avoid not only pesticides, industrial contaminants, hormones, and antibiotics, but also nitrates and nitrites. Some natural food stores and food cooperatives carry organic pork products.

When cooking pork, the minimum temperature to attain is 160° F; for well done, cook to 170° F. Fresh ham should also be cooked to 160° F, while precooked ham can be heated to 140° F. Failing to cook pork properly can expose you to foodborne illness (see chapter 1).

Veal

The harsh and unusual conditions under which veal is produced make it very susceptible to contamination, especially from drugs. Veal calves are confined to crates that do not permit them to enjoy natural movement but do expose them to pain, disease, and deprivation. Veal calves, for example, are often kept in complete darkness and are nearly completely denied solid food. Instead, they are forced to drink a liquid, drug-laden feed ("milk-fed veal") designed to stimulate growth and help prevent disease. These calves often suffer from chronic diarrhea and experience many gastrointestinal and respiratory diseases, which must be treated with massive amounts of drugs. It is uncertain that the drugs forced upon these calves are adequately cleared from the animals' systems before they are slaughtered, which means they may be in the veal you eat.

There is also concern that the illegal drug clenbuterol, which stimulates growth of lean muscle in calves, may be present in some veal. Individuals who eat meat that has been tainted with clenbuterol may experience respiratory arrest.

Safety Hints. Veal is not a recommended meat choice, both because of the toxin residues in the meat and the inhumane ways the calves are treated. If, however, you decide to eat veal, look for organically, humanely raised veal, which is available from a limited number of suppliers. Calves raised in this manner are not given additives, hormones, or drugs, and they are allowed to feed naturally from their mothers. Organically raised veal looks more like beef than the pale, "milk-fed" veal with which you may be familiar.

When cooking veal, allow it to reach a minimum temperature of 160° F, which should be checked with a meat thermometer.

CHAPTER 12

Poultry

Americans are eating more poultry. As beef consumption dropped steadily, from peak consumption of around 90 pounds per person per year in the mid-1970s to about 62 pounds in 2000, intake of chicken and turkey rose. Chicken consumption increased from 25 pounds per person per year in 1970 to 54 pounds in 1999; turkey rose from 6.4 pounds to 14.2. Much of this increase in poultry consumption is attributed to concern for the high fat and cholesterol content in red meat. However, poultry has similar, and in some cases higher, amounts of cholesterol than some beef. For example, three ounces of turkey leg without skin has 101 mg of cholesterol, more than found in three ounces of ground beef, lean beef chuck blade, or lean beef rib. Three ounces of chicken breast without skin has just four less milligrams of cholesterol (64 mg) than the same amount of lean beef rib. Duck and goose equal or surpass several types of beef in cholesterol levels.

That being said, should you decide to make poultry a part of your family's diet, you should know the safest ways to choose, store, and prepare it.

Here are the general safety guidelines for handling poultry:

- When buying poultry, place the packages in separate plastic bags so raw juices, which contain bacteria, won't contaminate other foods.

- Refrigerate or freeze poultry as soon as you get home, because bacteria multiply rapidly at room temperature.
- When handling raw poultry, first wash your hands with soap and hot water to avoid cross-contamination from other foods or objects you have touched, and wash them again when you are done handling the poultry.
- Use a plastic cutting board for poultry, because bacteria can take up residence in the grooves of wooden ones. When you've finished using the cutting board, wash it and any utensils you used to prepare the poultry with hot water and soap.
- Remove the skin from poultry before you cook it, because many pesticides accumulate there.
- If you are going to stuff poultry, do so immediately before you roast it, not the day or night before. When the poultry is done, remove the stuffing immediately. The cavity of poultry is a fertile environment for bacteria to breed.
- Do not eat the organs of poultry, because higher levels of toxins tend to accumulate there.
- Do not place cooked poultry on the same plate used for the raw poultry, as bacteria can be passed on to the cooked poultry.
- Thoroughly cook all poultry to the specified temperature (see individual instructions in the entries below). *Campylobacter jejuni*, bacteria that can cause severe diarrhea, nausea, vomiting, and headache, is most commonly caused by undercooked poultry.

LET'S GO SHOPPING

In this section we look at specific types of poultry and offer you guidelines on how to identify and purchase the

safest varieties for your family and how to store and
prepare them. When we refer to the FDA's pesticide
monitoring program or Total Diet Study, or to the
USDA's Pesticide Data Program, we are referring to
2001 report results. For more information about various
pesticides mentioned in the entries, refer to chapter 2
and the Appendix; for more on industrial contaminants,
see chapter 4.

Chicken

Americans love chicken: According to the USDA Economic Research Service, from 1980 to 2000 chicken consumption rose 62 percent, from 33 pounds per person to
53 pounds. If you are like many Americans who are
eating chicken more often, you need to consider the possible health risks associated with eating it, including exposure to antibiotics, pesticides, and disease-causing
organisms.

Antibiotics. Antibiotics are routinely fed to chickens
to make them produce more meat and to help ward off
the many bacterial diseases that are spread throughout
the greatly overcrowded conditions under which chickens
are kept. (Even so-called free-range chickens exist in
vastly overcrowded conditions, because the guidelines for
free-range chickens are not enforced.) These antibiotics
are then found in the chicken you eat. As we noted in
chapter 4, the more antibiotics you ingest, the more bacteria become resistant to these drugs, and the less effective antibiotics become when you need them to treat a
bacterial illness.

Pesticides. The pesticides you ingest from eating
chicken originally come from the feed the chickens eat.
Pesticides tend to accumulate in fat, so you can expect
to find higher levels of pesticides in the skin, dark meat,
and organs. Health risks associated with the pesticides
fed to chickens include cancer, nervous system damage,
birth defects, and other problems.

One of the pesticides found in chicken feed—arsenic, used to control intestinal parasites—is a known carcinogen, and has recently raised concerns among experts. According to a study published in January 2004 in *Environmental Health Perspectives,* the levels of arsenic found in chicken are contributing a significant amount to people's total arsenic exposure. The study indicates that the mean level of chicken consumption exposes people to 3.6 to 5.2 micrograms per day of arsenic. Given that we are exposed to arsenic in drinking water, fumes, dust, and other foods in the diet, the combination from all these sources may present a health problem for some people. Chronic exposure to arsenic (10 to 40 micrograms per day) is associated with respiratory, bladder, and skin cancers.

The Total Diet Study looks at various types of chicken products and analyzes them for pesticide residues and industrial contaminants. For example, chicken nuggets sampled from fast-food establishments revealed evidence of the industrial contaminants benzene and styrene (carcinogens), chloroform (probable carcinogen), toluene, and xylene, and the pesticides chlorpyrifos and malathion (can damage the nervous system). Fried chicken tested in the Total Diet Study had traces of dieldrin (may cause nervous system damage, cancer, and birth defects). Samples of chicken potpie (heated) had traces of chlorpropham (may cause tumors).

Safety Hints. Thaw frozen chicken in the refrigerator overnight. If you need to thaw it quickly, place the frozen chicken in a plastic bag, seal it well, and immerse it in cold water for about an hour. If you have a microwave, you can put the frozen chicken into a microwavable casserole and defrost it in the microwave.

When cooking chicken, use a meat thermometer to check for doneness. A whole chicken or thighs should reach 180° F; breasts, 170° F; and ground chicken, 165° F.

To help prevent foodborne illnesses, chicken should be handled according to the guidelines presented at the beginning of this chapter. To minimize your exposure to antibiotics and pesticides, including arsenic, buy organic chicken, which is available at many natural food stores and food cooperatives, and some farmers' markets.

Duck

Domestically raised ducks can be exposed to pesticides in their feed, as well as drugs administered to help ward off or treat disease. Ducks can also carry *Listeria monocytogenes*, which causes a foodborne disease called listeriosis that can be dangerous for the very young, the elderly, and people who have chronic diseases (see chapter 1). Duck meat has been the subject of several recalls, including two in 2001: one for 4,400 pounds and another for 780 pounds, both for listeria contamination. Duck meat production has also been a topic of controversy, as the conditions under which ducks are raised are usually cruel, including severe overcrowding and debilling so the ducks cannot engage in natural behaviors. Such cruelty was a reason the supermarket chain Trader Joe's stopped selling duck meat in 2001.

Safety Hints. Meat from domestically raised ducks is generally safer than that from those caught in the wild, as the latter are often exposed to a variety of pesticides in their food and water, and hunters who eat their catches have no way of knowing which toxins are in the fowl. If you want to include duck in your diet, limit it to organically raised duck, which can be found in some natural food stores or food cooperatives, as well as online. Cook duck until it reaches a temperature of 180° F; check with a meat thermometer.

Goose

Goose is not a common choice among poultry eaters in the United States. However, some people do hunt geese and may believe they are exposed to fewer pesticides from wild than from domesticated geese. Unfortunately, this is not necessarily true, as geese can ingest pesticides in many forms from the environment, and hunters have no way of knowing the toxic levels in the geese they kill.

The FDA forbids the use of hormones in domestically raised geese, and few drugs have been approved for use as well. If drugs are given to geese as treatment for an illness, they cannot be slaughtered for a specific period of time. Time allows drug levels in the meat to decline.

Processed Products. Goose liver, also known as foie gras, is the product of an extremely cruel process in which geese are force-fed corn mush through a long funnel that is forced down their necks. This forced feeding makes the liver incapable of functioning, and it becomes enlarged. Foie gras is extremely high in cholesterol: one 3.5-ounce serving contains more than 150 percent of the average person's daily cholesterol limit.

Safety Hints. To minimize your exposure to pesticides and other contaminants, choose organically raised rather than wild or conventionally raised goose. When cooking goose, allow the internal temperature to reach 180° F (use a meat thermometer).

Turkey

According to the USDA Economic Research Service, consumption of turkey in the United States has risen by a larger percentage than chicken. From 1980 to 2000, turkey consumption rose 68 percent, from an average of 8 pounds per person per year to 14 pounds.

Traces of DDE (possible carcinogen) were found in samples of roasted turkey breast in the Total Diet Study. The only other turkey samples taken in the study were for a turkey frozen dinner that also included dressing, gravy, potatoes, and vegetables. Pesticide residues detected in these meals included endosulfan (may cause birth defects, cancer, nervous system damage), malathion (can cause nervous system damage), and chlorpropham (may cause tumors).

Safety Hints. When preparing turkey, it is best to begin with meat that is completely thawed. A frozen or partially thawed turkey will take up to twice as long to cook thoroughly as a thawed one. An unstuffed, 8-to-12 pound turkey should take 2.75 to 3 hours to roast, while a 20-to-24 pound turkey should take 4.5 to 5 hours. If the turkey is stuffed, allow 3 to 3.5 hours for an 8-to-12 pound turkey and 4.75 to 5.25 hours for a 20-to-24 pound turkey.

Always use a meat thermometer to check the internal temperature of the turkey. If the turkey is stuffed, the internal temperature of the stuffing should be 165° F, while the temperature of the whole turkey must reach 180° F in the innermost part of the thigh. Ground turkey should reach 165° F.

CHAPTER 13

Fish and Shellfish

You hear it or read about it all the time: Eat more fish. Fish is a health food. The American Heart Association recommends that people eat fish twice a week. And people may be listening. The USDA Economic Research Service reports that consumption of fish and shellfish in the United States has been on the rise: From 1980 to 2000, consumption increased 23 percent, from 12 pounds per person per year to 15 pounds.

But you also hear stories about contaminated fish and how pregnant women and young children should be careful when choosing fish. So what's the truth? Is fish really good for your heart and brain, or is that just a fish story? If you eat fish while pregnant, will you place your unborn child in danger? What kinds of fish are safe to eat? Should you feed your three-year-old fish sticks? How concerned should you be about mercury, dioxins, and other toxins in fish? Is fish raised on fish farms safer than fish caught in the wild?

The controversy and debate about the safety of fish and shellfish can be confusing. Added to this confusion is the fact that there is no mandated inspection of seafood by the federal government, so you as a consumer must be vigilant when making a seafood purchase. In this chapter we bring you the latest information to help you answer your concerns so you can make your own decisions about including or excluding fish from your diet.

THE FISH STORY

When people talk about the health benefits of fish, one of the phrases you'll often hear is "omega-3 fatty acids." These essential nutrients are critical for proper development of the fetal brain, and they've also been associated with reducing the symptoms or occurrence of arthritis, cramps, headache, heart attack, Alzheimer's disease, and autoimmune conditions. Fish that are the richest sources of omega-3 fatty acids include salmon (wild), tuna (steaks; canned has less), rainbow trout, sardines, herring, and pilchard.

The downside of the fish story is the contaminants: specifically, mercury, polychlorinated biphenyls (PCBs), and other pesticides. While these toxins are of concern for everyone, they are of particular importance to women who may become pregnant, pregnant and nursing women, and young children.

Is Fish Safe for Young Children and Pregnant Women?

About 8 percent of women in the United States who are of childbearing age have enough mercury in their blood to put their fetus at risk for birth defects. One of the main sources of that mercury is fish, with the ever-popular tuna likely topping the list. This is a cause for concern for several reasons.

For example, results of FDA tests reported in December 2003 showed that albacore "white" canned tuna contains almost three times as much mercury as cheaper, "light" canned tuna. This has led some consumer groups to urge women and young children to avoid albacore canned tuna. The FDA takes the stand that women should get their 12-ounce weekly quota of fish from several varieties of fish and not eat the same type of fish more than once a week. However, the FDA did not state exactly how much tuna, or any other variety of fish, is safe for women and children to eat. A woman who weighs 100 pounds can safely eat less than a woman who is, say, 150 pounds, yet the FDA has not offered consumers guidance on this issue. Similarly, the safe limits of certain fish for a 30-pound child will differ from those for an 85-pound child, yet the FDA only states that children should eat less than 12 ounces of fish. How much less?

Based on data from the EPA and the FDA, the Natural Resources Defense Council, a nonprofit organization of specialists dedicated to protecting public health and the environment, developed some recommendations for women and children who want to eat tuna (see entry for "Tuna" below).

On the plus side of the fish question is that certain fish (e.g., salmon, trout, sardines, herring) contain significant amounts of omega-3 fatty acids, which are critical for the healthy development of the brain, nervous tissue, and retina of a fetus. After birth, infants continue to require omega-3 fatty acids for these purposes, and an excellent source of these fatty acids can be breast milk. During pregnancy, fatty acids are transferred through the placenta to the fetus, and during breastfeeding they are transported via breast milk. To ensure that the fetus and infant get the necessary omega-3 fatty acids, women who are pregnant as well as those who are nursing need to consume foods that contain them, such as fish, leafy green vegetables, and nuts.

Transported along with the omega-3 fatty acids, however, can be contaminants found in fish, such as mercury, PCBs, and pesticide residues, which can damage the developing brain and nervous system. If you are pregnant or breastfeeding, you should avoid albacore canned tuna, as already mentioned, as well as predator fish and fish that live for many years, such as shark, swordfish, king mackerel, marlin, and tilefish, as these fish typically have high levels of mercury and other toxins. Generally, it is also best to avoid fish caught in local lakes or streams, as they are more likely to be contaminated. Pregnant and lactating women and children should always avoid eating raw fish and shellfish, which often carry parasites and other organisms that can cause serious illness.

Cooking fish can reduce the PCB levels if the fat is allowed to drain off as it cooks (PCBs accumulate in fat), but it does not affect mercury levels, because mercury is distributed throughout the fish.

Another consideration is allergies. Parents who are allergic to seafood, pollen, or bee stings should not give seafood (e.g., crab, crayfish, lobster, shrimp) to children younger than age three, as the children are susceptible to developing these allergies as well.

Going Fishing?

If you want to include fish in your diet and you also like to go fishing, you may want to practice throwing those fish back, take up hiking as your new outdoor sport, and then head to your local fish store. Many lakes and streams in the United States are contaminated with a variety of pollutants, including PCBs, DDT, and other dangerous pesticides. That means the fish swimming in those waterways are contaminated as well.

Take Lake Michigan, for example. A study published in *Environmental Health Perspectives* showed that among people older than 49, many former big eaters of fish caught in the lake now have high levels of PCBs in their blood and problems with memory and learning. Dozens of other studies show that eating contaminated fish from tainted waterways can result in health and learning problems for people of all ages.

In a study conducted by toxin expert Charles Santerre and his research team at Purdue University along with the US Department of Agriculture, investigators tested fish for more than three dozen different pesticides and found that wild-caught catfish, red swamp crayfish, and rainbow trout had higher levels of pesticides than the same types of fish raised on fish farms. This doesn't mean the farm-raised fish were pesticide-free; in fact, they contained the same pesticides, but at lower levels considered to be safe by the FDA.

If you still want to eat the fish you catch, you should check out the contamination level of the fishing hole. In waterways near the Great Lakes, for example, the PCB levels can be ten times higher than the acceptable level. The Environmental Protection Agency issues fishing advisories on lakes, rivers, and connecting waterways to inform consumers about whether it is safe to eat fish caught in certain areas. In 2002, for example, 2,800 advisories were issued, which represented about one-third of the nation's total lake area and more than 15 percent of the river miles. Advisories were also issued for waterways such as the Chesapeake Bay and Lake Champlain.

To check out the advisories, see the National Listing of Fish and Wildlife Advisories Web site at www.epa.gov/waterscience/fish or contact your local health department or state fishing advisory board. The Environmental Protection Agency also has an online listing at http:/fish.rti.org/ The states that traditionally have the most fishing advisories are Florida, Georgia, Indiana, Massachusetts, Michigan, Nebraska, New Jersey, Ohio, Texas, and Wisconsin.

Here are some general guidelines for safe fish consumption:

- Buy fish from reputable sources only. People who hawk "freshly caught fish" from the back of their trucks or coolers are not a good choice.
- When buying fresh seafood, make sure it has been refrigerated or frozen properly.
- If buying frozen fish and the package is transparent, look for signs of frost or crystals. Their presence could mean that the fish once was thawed and then refrozen.
- Do not buy cooked seafood or smoked fish if it is displayed in the same case as raw fish.
- When buying shellfish, choose those that have tightly closed shells.

- Do not buy shellfish that has a strong "fishy" odor, because it is likely spoiled.
- Refrigerate or freeze fish immediately when you get it home from the store. You may want to bring a small ice chest with you in the car to keep fish and seafood (and other perishable items) safe while transporting them home.
- Rinse and rewrap fish when you get it home. Place it on paper towels, put it in a plastic bag or tightly covered container, and place it in the coldest part of the refrigerator or in a pan of ice.
- Before cooking the fish, remove the skin and remove any fatty tissue from the belly, side, and along the top of the back. These are areas where toxins accumulate. Also remove the liver, which is a storage area for contaminants.
- Prepare the fish in ways that allow any fat to drip away: broil, barbecue, or bake.
- Throw away fat drippings from boiled or poached fish. Toxins accumulate in fat.
- Mercury accumulates mainly in the muscle (fillets) of fish and thus can't be removed. To minimize exposure, eat smaller, younger fish that are known to have minimal or low levels of mercury, and eat fish from a variety of water bodies to reduce your risk of heavy exposure to any one or more toxins in addition to mercury that are found in some fish. If you want to know how much mercury is found in many different varieties of fish, visit the following Web site: www.cfsan.fda.gov/~frf/sea-mehg.html
- Raw fish and seafood isn't recommended for anyone, but especially if you have certain medical conditions, because the condition and/or the medications taken for them may put you at risk for serious illness or death if you eat contaminated fish. Those conditions include cancer, liver disease, diabetes, HIV/AIDS, low stomach acid or history of stomach surgery, long-term steroid use, and hemochromatosis (an iron disorder).
- Fish and seafood should be cooked until the internal

temperature is at least 145° F. The safe temperature for fish cakes and other flaked or ground fish is 155° F, and for stuffed fish, at least 165° F.

- If you don't have a meat thermometer, you can check for fish and seafood doneness using the following tips. For fish, use the tip of a sharp knife to penetrate the flesh and pull it aside. If the flakes are beginning to separate, the edges are opaque, and the center is translucent, allow the fish to cook for another three to four minutes. With seafood, lobster and shrimp turn red and the flesh becomes pearly opaque; scallops turn white or opaque and are firm; clams, mussels, and oysters open up. Any that stay closed should be thrown away.

LET'S GO SHOPPING

The FDA's pesticide monitoring program found that 29 percent of domestic and 5.8 percent of imported fish and shellfish had pesticide residues. Unfortunately, mercury levels are not checked as part of this program. Mercury levels are investigated by the EPA and by individual states' environmental protection departments, which issue advisories on fish and shellfish safety (see "Going Fishing?").

In this section we'll look at some specific types of fish and shellfish and what you need to know to make safe, nutritious choices for you and your family, whether you eat fish at home or in a restaurant. Speaking of eating out, the Total Diet Study sampled fish sandwiches from fast-food establishments. These fish pieces typically contain several different types of fish, but they also contain, according to the study, residues of DDE, DDT, dieldrin, malathion, chlorpropham, and chlorpyrifos.

Catfish

According to the National Fisheries Institute (2001 results), catfish is the fifth most consumed fish in the

United States: 1.103 pounds per person. Catfish (typically channel catfish) are also the number two farmed fish in the United States, so chances are strong that the catfish you buy at the store or in a restaurant has come from a catfish farm. This is good news, because wild catfish are often contaminated with cancer-causing dioxins, PCBs, heptachlor, and brain-damaging mercury, among other toxins. In fact, fishing advisories for catfish are common and have been, and continue to be, issued by dozens of states. Farmed catfish are not toxin-free, however, as drugs are used in their feed to ward off disease and thus can be found in the flesh of the catfish you eat.

Safety Hints. Before fishing for catfish, check for fishing advisories for the waters in which you plan to fish. A safer choice would be to purchase farmed channel catfish, but you should broil or grill it to allow toxins in the fat to drip away. The Environmental Working Group and Public Interest Research Groups recommend that pregnant women eat no more than one meal per month of wild catfish, but they can eat farmed catfish more often.

Clams

Clams are the eighth most popular fish/seafood consumed in the United States: 0.545 pounds per person per year. Clams are likely to contain contaminants from the waters in which they live, including dioxins, PCBs, heptachlor, and industrial toxins.

Clams are highly susceptible to bacterial contamination. If you eat undercooked or raw contaminated clams, you may develop gastroenteritis, which is characterized by severe diarrhea, vomiting, and stomach cramps. You also risk developing infectious hepatitis (inflammation of the liver), a potentially fatal disease. Yet another risk associated with clams is paralytic shellfish poisoning, which is caused by red tides—minute poisonous organisms that occasionally invade various coastal areas and infect clams. The condition is so named because after suffering nausea, vomiting, and numbness less than an hour after eating contaminated clams, individuals can experience paralysis and breathing problems.

Safety Hints. In some states, the National Shellfish Sanitation Program monitors the harvest of clams for safety and tags them. If you buy clams from a fish dealer, he should show you the tag; packaged clams should have a sticker from the state agency.

Live clams should have tightly closed shells; don't buy clams that have cracked or open shells. Freshly shucked clams should smell briny and have no trace of ammonia. Store live clams in the refrigerator covered with wet towels, not in an airtight container or in water. They should keep four to seven days. Be sure to immediately remove any clams that die, because they can contaminate the others. Store shucked clams immersed in their liquid in tightly covered containers, which should keep them viable for up to one week. Most raw or cooked clams can be kept for two months in a 0° F freezer. Thaw them in the refrigerator.

If you shuck your own clams, scrub the shells with a stiff brush and rinse under cold running water. To loosen grit in the clams, soak them in salt water—two teaspoons of salt to a gallon of water—and let the clams sit in this solution for two to three hours.

Steaming destroys most bacteria in clams, but the organisms that cause paralytic shellfish poisoning are not affected. Eating raw clams is strongly discouraged for everyone, but young children, the elderly, and people who have a compromised immune system should never eat them.

Crab

The National Fisheries Institute identified crab as the seventh most popular fish/seafood choice among Americans, who eat an average of 0.568 pounds of the crustaceans per person per year.

The safety of the crabs you eat depends on where

they were harvested and how well they are prepared. In November 2003, for example, crabs from the Newark Bay in New Jersey were identified as exposing people to cancer risk levels as much as a million times what the EPA considers to be safe. The offending toxin was 2,3,7,8-TCDD, the most toxic form of dioxin, which was being dumped into the water by a nearby plant. Other fish and shellfish in the bay, including lobster, were also contaminated.

Other fishing spots have also been identified as being contaminated to such a level that crab and other marine life are affected, such as the Chesapeake Bay and Houston Channel area.

Safety Hints. There are hundreds of species of crabs, but in the United States, the most popular are blue (from the Atlantic coast), Dungeness (northwest coast), king (north Pacific Ocean), snow (Atlantic and Pacific), and stone (Florida and Texas). You should buy crab only from reliable vendors; do not trust roadside sellers. If you are harvesting your own crabs, check the fishing advisories in the area for any warnings (see "Going Fishing?").

Fresh cooked crab smells clean, without any ammonia odor, and the shells are bright. Exposed meat should be moist and white. It is best to eat freshly cooked crab the same day it is cooked, but it will keep for up to two days in the refrigerator if tightly covered or for up to two months in the freezer. Keep pasteurized crabmeat in the refrigerator for up to six months unopened, but use it within four days after opening the package.

If you handle live crabs, wear fishing or other heavy gloves. Blood poisoning can develop from being pinched by crabs, because many bacteria live on their shells.

Lobster

Most of the lobsters consumed in the United States come from Maine (Maine lobster), the Pacific Ocean and waters in the southeast (spiny or rock lobster), or from

Australia, New Zealand, or South Africa. Lobsters may be contaminated with PCBs, dioxins, or other industrial contaminants, depending on where they are harvested (see "Crabs").

Safety Hints. Lobster livers, or "tomalleys," are considered a delicacy by some people, but they are especially high in toxins and should be avoided. Eating a contaminated tomalley can cause paralytic shellfish poisoning, with symptoms that include numbness of the lips, dizziness, nausea, vomiting, breathing difficulties, and choking.

Buy fresh lobster from reliable markets only; avoid roadside vendors. Freshly cooked lobster has a bright red shell, and the meat is moist and white. It is best to eat freshly cooked lobster the same day it is prepared, but it will keep for up to two days in the refrigerator if tightly covered or for up to two months in the freezer.

Pollock

Alaska pollock is the fourth most popular fish/shellfish consumed in the United States: 1.13 pounds per person per year. If the name "pollock" doesn't sound familiar, "fish sticks" probably does. Pollock, or more specifically, Alaska pollock, is the fish used in fish sticks, the fish in fish and chips, and the ingredient in surimi (mock crabmeat). In the Total Diet Study, fish sticks were found to contain chlorpyrifos-methyl and malathion, along with the industrial contaminants chloroform, styrene, toluene, and xylene.

Safety Hints. While Alaska pollock is generally considered to have little contamination with heavy metals, PCBs, dioxins, or pesticides, Atlantic pollock presents a higher risk. Therefore, look for ALASKA POLLOCK on the ingredient label or when buying fresh pollock. Follow the safety guidelines as outlined at the beginning of this chapter.

Salmon

One of the most popular fish in the United States (fourth on the list of top ten) is salmon. Salmon is a "fatty" fish, and of all the types of fatty fish it is one of the best sources of omega-3 fatty acids. However, according to a US Department of Agriculture study (2002), farmed salmon contains an average of 35 percent less omega-3 fatty acids than wild-caught salmon.

Farmed vs. Wild Salmon. If the word "salmon" conjures up an image of fish leaping into the air and fighting their way upstream, you may be surprised to learn that about 60 percent of all the salmon eaten in the United States comes from fish farms, and the percentage continues to rise. If you're thinking that farmed salmon are probably much safer than salmon caught in the wild, several recent studies indicate otherwise.

A study published in January 2004 in *Science* reported that levels of PCBs (polycholorinated biphenyls, which accumulate in the body and affect hormone function; see chapter 4), dioxins, dieldrin, and toxaphene were higher in farmed salmon than in the wild variety, and noted that farmed salmon from Europe were more contaminated than those produced in North America.

An earlier study (July 2003) conducted by the Environmental Working Group had also found that much of the farmed salmon sold in the United States contains high levels of PCBs, and noted that the reason is because farmed salmon are fed food that is contaminated with this industrial toxin. This practice, along with the fact that farmed salmon are intentionally fattened to maximize profits, results in an ounce of farmed salmon that contains 52 percent more fat than an ounce of wild salmon.

Because PCBs accumulate in fat, farmed salmon contain higher levels of the toxin than do wild salmon. Studies show that the average level of PCBs in farmed salmon is 5 to 10 times that of wild salmon. Scientists have also found that farmed salmon contains higher levels of many other contaminants, including flame retardants, DDT, dieldrin, and carcinogenic substances called polynuclear aromatic hydrocarbons (PAHs). The Total Diet Study found chlordane, DDE, dieldrin, heptachlor, hexachlorobenzene, PCBs, and pentachlorobenzene in its samples of salmon steaks and fillets.

Yet another factor to consider in the wild versus farmed salmon question is that two different agencies set the safety standards for salmon: the FDA for farmed salmon (because they are raised, like livestock), and the EPA for wild salmon (because they are a direct product of the environment). The FDA's standards are 500 times less protective than those of the EPA, which means wild salmon that meets EPA standards is significantly safer than farmed salmon that meets FDA criteria.

Safety Hints. In the *Science* article mentioned above, the Environmental Working Group noted that consumers should choose wild over farmed salmon, and made the following recommendations for salmon consumption: Per month, individuals should eat no more than approximately four to eight ounces of European farmed salmon, and no more than about one pound total of US farmed salmon. Wild salmon from Alaska (Pacific salmon) is considered to be the safest salmon, followed by Atlantic salmon. Salmon caught in inland waterways (e.g., coho salmon), like the Great Lakes or rivers, are more contaminated with the substances already mentioned.

Salmon should be baked, broiled, or grilled, and the fat should be allowed to drip away from the fish and then discarded. See other guidelines for handling fish and shellfish at the beginning of this chapter.

Scallops

Scallops are number ten on the list of top ten fish/shellfish consumed in the United States, according to the National Fisheries Institute (2000). Scallops come in two main varieties: bay scallops, which are usually caught in the shallow water in the northeast and in Gulf coastal waters; and sea scallops, which are harvested in deeper water. The latter are more common and less expensive. Scallops are subject to contamination by PCBs, dioxins, heptachlor, and other toxins, depending on where they are gathered.

Safety Hints. Buy scallops only from reputable vendors. Fresh scallops smell slightly sweet, not fishy. Because scallops are highly perishable, they should be refrigerated at the selling point, and you should keep them cold until you are ready to cook them, preferably the same day you buy them.

You need to cook scallops to 145° F to kill microorganisms, some of which can cause infectious hepatitis—a potentially fatal disease characterized by inflammation of the liver—or gastroenteritis, which is characterized by diarrhea, severe stomach cramps, and vomiting. If you want to freeze scallops, cook them first, then put them in an airtight container. They will keep up to two months at 0° F. See other guidelines for handling fish/shellfish at the beginning of this chapter.

Shrimp

Shrimp is second only to tuna in the top ten fish/shellfish Americans eat. According to the National Marine Fisheries Service, Americans eat an average of 3.2 pounds of shrimp per person per year. The Environmental Working Group and Public Interest Research Groups have identified shrimp as one of the safer fish/shellfish to eat, but they also note that shrimp harvesting practices have a severe negative impact on the environment. The Total Diet Study analyzed samples of shrimp and found DDE and atrazine (linked to prostate cancer; see Appendix). Shrimp also has higher cholesterol levels than any other seafood (166 mg per three-ounce serving).

Safety Hints. If you buy fresh shrimp, it should have a gray-greenish color, be firm with a clean smell (no ammonia), and be cold. You can store uncooked shrimp in the refrigerator, but it is best to cook it the same day you purchase it. If you want to freeze fresh shrimp, cook it first. Both frozen fresh shrimp and shrimp you buy already frozen will keep about two months at 0° F.

It is important to cook shrimp sufficiently to kill any microorganisms. Properly cooked shrimp should be pink or orange.

Tuna

Tuna is the number one fish consumed in the United States: According to the National Fisheries Institute, average consumption of tuna is 3.6 pounds per person per year. That includes canned as well as tuna steaks.

In the Total Diet Study, samples of canned tuna revealed the industrial contaminants benzene (carcinogen), chloroform and DDE (probable carcinogens), toluene, and xylene. Samples of tuna casserole that were analyzed were found to contain DDE (probable carcinogen); chlorpyrifos, dicloran, and dieldrin (can cause nervous system damage), and permethrin (possible carcinogen). Mercury is not tested in this study. However, as mentioned under "Is Fish Safe for Young Children and Pregnant Women?", mercury is a serious concern, especially for these two groups, who should limit their consumption of tuna.

Another concern with tuna is scromboid, a type of food poisoning caused by eating certain fish—like tuna—that contain high amounts of histamine and that have begun to spoil. (Mahimahi, mackerel, and sardines are some others.) Improper handling, storage, and preparation of tuna can cause this problem. Scromboid poisoning is characterized by facial flush, sweating, nausea, dizziness, and headache, and can lead to respiratory distress and swollen tongue.

Safety Hints. Because the EPA has not given any definitive guidelines on how much tuna is safe for young children and pregnant women to eat, the Natural Resources Defense Council analyzed the data from the

EPA and devised its own guidelines for these individuals. These amounts are based on the safety limits established by the EPA.

Table 5

Person's Weight	# 6-oz Cans Albacore	# 6-oz Cans Light Tuna
44 lb child	1 can every 4 weeks	1 can every 12 days
66 lb child	1 can every 3 weeks	1 can every 8 days
110 lb woman	1 can every 12 days	1 can every 5 days
143 lb woman	1 can every 9 days	1 can every 4 days
209 lb woman	1 can every 6 days	1 can every 2 days

In March 2004, the FDA and EPA modified their recommendations about albacore tuna, stating that women and children can choose to eat up to six ounces of albacore tuna per week. Again, they did not give a breakdown based on weight, and so the safety limits given in the table still hold.

CHAPTER 14

Eggs and Dairy Products

According to the FDA's pesticide monitoring program, milk, dairy products, and eggs are among the safest foods when it comes to pesticide residues. The 2001 figures show that 97 percent of domestic and 100 percent of imported products were pesticide-free.

That's the good news. The not-so-good news is that most dairy cows are given antibiotics and hormones that are passed along into their milk, which results in contaminated milk and dairy products. You also need to consider possible foodborne illnesses that can be caused by improper handling, storage, or preparation of these foods. In fact, when it comes to eggs, the most important issue is foodborne problems associated with the bacteria salmonella, as well as improper storage and preparation.

In this chapter we discuss how you can ensure that you and your family will enjoy safe dairy products and eggs.

EGGS

When asked what they think about eggs and health, many people think first of cholesterol, as egg consumption has been associated with hardening of the arteries, heart attack, and stroke. Yet you also need to think about safety when you buy and prepare eggs for your

family, whether you are making a dish that features eggs
(e.g., an omelet or scrambled eggs) or adding them to
cake batter or potato salad.

The Incredibly Fragile, Tough Egg

If you hold an egg in your hand, you know that if you
gently squeeze it you will end up with a gooey mess in
your hand. Yet nature has created a surprisingly strong
protection for a developing chick. An eggshell is com-
posed of two layers—an outer protein film called the
cuticle and a calcium carbonate shell—and the yolk and
white are encased in a membrane. The cuticle prevents
microorganisms and moisture from penetrating the inner
layer of the shell, which is porous.

When eggs are collected, they are "candled" to make
sure they are free of a developing chick or blood clots,
and then they are cleaned. In some cases, a thin layer of
mineral oil is applied to the shell to protect against the
cuticle drying out. A dry cuticle is susceptible to contamination by bacteria.

Salmonella Enteritidis

Bacteria called *Salmonella enteritidis* are one of two
main contaminants that can affect eggs. If you eat eggs
contaminated with these bacteria, you may develop salmonellosis, an illness that is characterized by severe diarrhea, headache, abdominal pain and cramps, fever, and,
in severe cases, death. You can avoid getting salmonellosis if you make sure you cook eggs until the yolks
have hardened; raw or undercooked eggs are havens
for salmonella.

According to the Centers for Disease Control and Prevention (CDC), there were 677 salmonellosis outbreaks
associated with *Salmonella enteritidis* from 1990 to 2001.
These outbreaks caused 23,366 people to get ill, 1,988
to require hospitalization, and 33 to die. One outbreak
involved nearly 100 students in Fort Monmouth, New
Jersey, who ate homemade ice cream made with raw

eggs. Another outbreak involved tainted tuna salad made with eggs.

Salmonella can be found on the outside of eggshells, which is why eggs are washed during processing. But the bacteria can also thrive inside uncracked, clean eggs if the hen had the infection. Salmonella doesn't make hens sick, but the bacteria can contaminate the yolk.

Salmonella is a major problem in dried egg powder, which is used in products such as cake mixes and pancake mixes. Dried egg powder is vigorously checked for contamination, and often large amounts of the powder are rejected because of contamination.

It is estimated that 1 out of every 10,000 eggs, or about 4.5 million eggs per year, are infected with *Salmonella enteritidis*, and that the majority of cases of salmonellosis come from infected hens (and thus the inside of the eggs are contaminated) and not from contaminated eggshells. Unfortunately, eggs that are contaminated with salmonella do not look or smell any different than eggs that are not contaminated, so you will not know if any of the eggs in your refrigerator are affected.

Free-Range Eggs

If you've seen egg cartons in the supermarket with the words "free-range eggs" stamped on them, you may have had visions in your mind of chickens roaming free in a spacious barnyard, pecking under a sunny sky. Unfortunately, "free-range" is basically a meaningless phrase. In most cases, it means that egg producers keep their hens either uncaged but confined to overly crowded sheds with perhaps one small door at one end through which a few hens may escape outside, or confined to cages that are bit larger than those used to hold battery-caged hens. There are no government laws or standards that regulate the meaning of "free-range" or "free-roaming" on egg cartons. Unless you can see the conditions under which the eggs are produced—perhaps you purchase free-range eggs from a local farmer—you do not know how the chickens are treated, and you may be paying more for nothing and supporting a cruel industry as well.

DAIRY PRODUCTS

In terms of pesticide contamination, dairy products in the United States appear to be safe: only 3 percent of domestic and 0 percent of imported dairy products had evidence of pesticide residues, according to the FDA's pesticide monitoring program. Other substances that may contaminate dairy products include antibiotics, hormones, and drugs, which are given to the vast majority of dairy cows, and which can affect your health and that of your family (see chapter 4). Dairy foods are also susceptible to contamination by microorganisms, which can cause foodborne illnesses. Yet one more consideration is the saturated fat and cholesterol content of many dairy products, substances that are linked with heart disease, stroke, diabetes, and other serious health problems.

That being said, there are choices you can make that will help ensure you and your family eat safe dairy products. Here are some common dairy foods and tips on how to make informed choices.

LET'S GO SHOPPING

Butter

Butter was named one of the top ten most contaminated foods by the Pesticide Action Network of North America and Commonweal, which came to this conclusion after analyzing EPA data. Butter is a high-fat food (at least 80 percent), and pesticides accumulate in fat. Pesticide residues found in butter reflect those that were in the milk from which it was made. According to the 2001 Total Diet Study, residues of DDE (possible carcinogen), dieldrin and endosulfan (can cause nervous system damage), industrial contaminants toluene, chloroform, and tetrachloroethylene (probable carcinogens), PCBs, heptachlor, and other contaminants were found in regular butter (salted). In addition to pesticides, butter may contain antibiotics and hormones if it was made from treated cows.

Nutritionally, one tablespoon of butter has 12 grams of total fat, 7 grams of which are artery-clogging saturated fat, as well as 31 mg cholesterol and 100 calories.

Safety Hints. For overall safety and health, it is recommended that you find a substitute for butter; for example, use olive oil (source of healthy fat; see chapter 15) on bread and vegetables or use fat-free yogurt on your baked potato. If you decide to continue using butter, do so sparingly.

When choosing butter, look for the USDA grade shield, which means the butter has been tested and graded by government inspectors for quality and keeping ability. Grade AA butter is made from fresh sweet cream, has a delicate sweet flavor, and a creamy texture. Grade A butter is made from fresh cream and has a fairly smooth texture. You should store butter in its original wrapper or container because it can absorb flavors from other foods. Butter may contain the additive tartrazine, which can cause asthmatic symptoms in sensitive individuals (see chapter 4).

Butter may be kept in the freezer for six to nine months; do not freeze whipped butter, however.

Cheese

There are dozens of different kinds of cheese, including hard cheese (e.g., cheddar, Parmesan, provolone, Romano), soft cheese (e.g., Brie, Goat cheeses, Camembert, Explorateur), and processed cheese (e.g., American, Velveeta). Pesticide residues found in cheese reflect those in the milk from which it was made. The high fat content of cheese also makes it amenable for pesticides to accumulate. The 2001 Total Diet Study found residues of chloroform (probable carcinogen), styrene (carcinogen), toluene, and xylene in cheddar cheese; the same residues plus DDE (possible carcinogen) and dieldrin (can cause nervous system damage) in Swiss cheese; and all the aforementioned residues plus tetrachloroethylene (probable carcinogen) and benzene in American processed cheese. Besides pesticides, cheeses can also contain antibiotics, hormones, and drugs that were given to the dairy cows.

Microorganisms that cause food poisoning are another concern with cheese. Listeria monocytogenes has been found in some soft-ripened cheeses, such as Brie and Camembert. Shredded cheese, which is more susceptible to moisture loss than blocks of cheese, is also more likely to develop mold.

Safety Hints. Look for "sell by" or "use by" dates on the package before you make your purchase. Hard cheese typically will keep for several weeks in the refrigerator if it is wrapped tightly. You can also freeze hard cheese; it is best to do so in pieces weighing one pound or less, or to grate it and store in an airtight bag. Thaw the cheese in the refrigerator before using it. Processed cheeses can be kept frozen for up to four months.

If mold develops on hard cheese, you can cut it off and eat the remaining, unaffected portion of the cheese. If you find mold on soft cheese, you should throw the cheese away, because the mold invades the entire piece of cheese, even if you can't see it. Blue cheeses, which are soft, are an exception, because the mold is safe to eat.

Processed cheeses are blends of cheeses that usually contain additives such as salt, artificial colors (e.g., tartrazine, which can cause asthmatic symptoms in sensitive people), preservatives, and other substances. If the label says "processed cheese food," the item may also include whey, water, and nonfat dry milk, which lowers the fat content. Processed cheese products are usually sold as slices or loaves or in jars.

Cottage Cheese

Cottage cheese is a soft, uncured cheese that is made by mixing dry curd cottage cheese with a creaming mixture. Dry curd cottage cheese has a milk fat content of less than 0.5 percent; cottage cheese must have at least 4 percent milk fat. Low-fat cottage cheese must have a milk fat content between 0.5 and 2 percent, while nonfat cottage cheese contains less than 0.5 percent total fat.

The Total Diet Study found DDE (possible carcinogen) in samples of 4 percent fat cottage cheese. Cottage cheese can be expected to contain the same pesticides, hormones, and antibiotics as the milk from which it was made. The additive carrageenan (see chapter 4), a suspected carcinogen, can be found in some brands of cottage cheese.

Safety Hints. Look for a "sell by" or "use by" date on the package before you make your purchase. Cottage cheese may have a USDA "Quality Approved" shield on the label if it was made under USDA supervision. However, absence of the shield does not mean the cottage cheese is not of good quality.

Use cottage cheese within ten to thirty days of purchase. You can freeze cottage cheese for up to three months. The consistency will change, but the taste should remain the same.

Cream Cheese

The 2001 Total Diet Study found traces of benzene, chloroform, DDE, dieldrin, toluene, and xylene in samples of cream cheese. Cream cheese can be expected to contain the same pesticides, hormones, and antibiotics as the milk from which it was made.

Safety Hints. Always check for a "sell by" or "use by" date on cream cheese before you purchase it. Cream cheese can be kept in the refrigerator for several weeks and in the freezer for up to three months. In the latter case, consistency will change, but the taste should remain the same.

Eggs

The Total Diet Study found residues of DDE (probable carcinogen) and the industrial contaminants chloroform (probable carcinogen), styrene (carcinogen),
toluene, and xylene in samples of scrambled eggs. Boiled
eggs revealed DDE.

Safety Hints. To protect yourself and your family
against salmonella poisoning, follow these guidelines
when purchasing, storing, and preparing eggs:

- Purchase eggs that are refrigerated at 40° F or
  lower.
- Look for eggs that have clean, uncracked shells.
- Look for a date on the egg carton. Don't buy out-
  of-date eggs.
- When you get the eggs home, put them in the refrigerator immediately. Place them in the coldest part
  of the refrigerator, not in the door.
- You can safely keep eggs in your refrigerator three
  to five weeks from the day you put them there, even
  if the "sell by" date expires during that time.
- Do not wash the eggs, as this could remove the
  protective coating and expose the eggs to
  contamination.
- If you accidentally crack an egg on the way home
  from the market or at home, break the egg into a
  clean container, cover it tightly, and keep it refrigerated. You should use it within two days.
- Make sure you cook all eggs completely, until the
  yolks and whites are firm (160° F). Do not eat
  sunny-side up eggs that are runny, lightly poached
  eggs, or soft-boiled eggs.
- Do not eat raw eggs or any items that contain raw
  eggs and that won't be cooked, such as homemade
  milk shakes, hollandaise sauce, homemade ice
  cream, or eggnog. Safe substitutes for raw eggs include liquid pasteurized egg products and pasteurized powdered egg whites.

- Do not leave eggs out of the refrigerator for longer than two hours.
- Serve cooked eggs or dishes that contain eggs immediately after cooking. If you don't use them right away, place them in shallow containers and refrigerate immediately. These dishes should be used within three to four days.
- If you make meringue, as in lemon meringue pie, bake it for fifteen minutes at 350°.
- To make sure dishes that contain eggs, such as quiches and casseroles, are sufficiently cooked, insert a food thermometer into the center of the food. A temperature of 160° F is safe.

Ice Cream

Ice cream contains 10 percent or more of milk fat, and this high fat content makes it a welcome environment for toxins to accumulate. Ice cream contains the pesticides and other residues that were in the milk from which it was made. That means hormones and antibiotics administered to dairy cows may be in the product, as well as pesticide residues and industrial contaminants. Some ice cream contains tartrazine, an artificial coloring that causes asthmatic symptoms in about 100,000 Americans. Another additive, carrageenan, a suspected carcinogen, is also found in some brands of ice cream (see chapter 4).

The Total Diet Study found evidence of DDE (possible carcinogen), as well as the industrial contaminants chloroform and tetrachloroethylene (probable carcinogens), and dieldrin (may cause nervous system damage, birth defects, cancer) in samples of vanilla ice cream. Samples of light vanilla ice cream also revealed benzene, chloroform, tetrachloroethylene, toluene, xylene, and bromodichloromethane (possible carcinogen). Hormone and antibiotic levels are not analyzed.

Safety Hints. To reduce your exposure to pesticides, hormones, and antibiotics, you can choose ice cream made from organic ingredients. Brands such as Horizon Organic and Stonyfield can be found in many supermarkets, as well as natural food stores and food cooperatives.

Milk

Milk consumption has been declining steadily for decades, says the USDA Economic Research Service. When it comes to whole milk, Americans were drinking an average of 25 gallons per person per year in 1970, but that number fell to only 8 gallons by 2000. Consumption of 2 percent milk rose from 3 gallons to just under 7 gallons during the same time period, while 1 percent milk struggled from less than 1 gallon to just over 2 and skim (fat-free) milk rose slightly from just under 2 to just under 4 gallons.

Milk can contain a variety of pesticides, hormones, antibiotics, and industrial contaminants. The Total Diet Study, for example, found residues of benzene and styrene (carcinogens), chloroform (probable carcinogen), DDE and dieldrin (may cause birth defects, cancer, nervous system damage), endosulfan (can cause nervous system damage), permethrin (possible carcinogen), and toluene in samples of whole milk. Samples of low-fat milk had DDE, dieldrin, and endosulfan residues, while skim milk revealed DDE residues.

Safety Hints. To avoid toxins, buy organic milk. Many supermarkets now carry organic varieties, as do natural food stores and food cooperatives.

When shopping for milk, it's good to know what you're getting:

- Vitamin D may be added to whole, low-fat, and skim milks. If vitamin D is added, the vitamin content must reach at least 400 IU per quart.
- Vitamin A is added to low-fat and skim milks to reach a level of at least 2,000 IU per quart.
- Milk can be labeled "Grade A" if it meets state or FDA standards for pasteurization. A Grade A rat-

ing means that the pasteurized milk came from healthy cows and that it was pasteurized under strict sanitary controls. It is not a statement about the quality of the milk.

- Whole milk must contain a minimum of 3.25 percent milk fat and 8.25 percent milk solids. It must also meet the minimum milk fat requirements set by the state in which it is sold. Whole milk is also usually homogenized and fortified with vitamin D.
- Low-fat milk contains 0.5 to 2 percent milkfat, 8.25 percent milk solids, and is fortified with vitamin A.

You can store milk in the freezer for up to one month. Leave room in the container for expansion. Thaw the milk in the refrigerator before use. The consistency of the milk will change, so it will be suitable for cooking only.

Sour Cream

According to the Total Diet Study, sour cream samples had evidence of dieldrin and hexachlorobenzene (may cause birth defects, cancer, nervous system damage), chloroform and lindane (probable carcinogens), DDE (possible carcinogen), and trichloroethylene. Sour cream can be expected to contain the same pesticides, antibiotics, and hormones as the milk from which it was made.

Safety Hints. Sour cream must contain at least 18 percent but less than 30 percent milk fat. It begins as light cream and can be soured in one of two ways: by adding a bacterial culture, which produces lactic acid, or by adding a food-grade acid. The latter must be labeled "acidified sour cream." The quality of both types of sour cream is the same.

Given that sour cream can be expected to contain the same pesticides, antibiotics, and hormones as the milk from which it was made, and that it is also high in fat and cholesterol, it is best to find a healthier alternative, such as plain, low-fat yogurt. If you do decide to use sour cream, look for low-fat, organic varieties (see Appendix).

Yogurt

The Total Diet Study did not find any pesticide residues in yogurt samples. However, yogurt can be expected to contain the same pesticides, antibiotics, and hormones as the milk from which it was made. Because toxins accumulate in fat, yogurts that are lower in fat also have lower levels of pesticides. Some brands of yogurt contain many additives, including artificial colors and flavors, artificial sweeteners, and preservatives. Tartrazine, an artificial color, is found in some yogurt and can cause asthmatic symptoms in some people (see chapter 4).

Safety Hints. The safest and healthiest yogurt is made with organic milk and contains no artificial additives. You can find organic yogurt in some supermarkets, as well as natural food stores and food cooperatives (also see Appendix).

CHAPTER 15

Oils and Fats

Oils and fats are a much misunderstood part of the American diet. You probably know that there are "good" fats that are beneficial for the heart and other bodily functions and "bad" fats that are detrimental for the heart, brain, intestinal tract, and other parts of the body. Our goal in this chapter is to tell you how to choose, store, and use oils and fats, and to encourage you to buy the good fats while minimizing or avoiding the bad ones.

WHAT ARE OILS AND FATS?

Oils and fats are substances that help make foods tasty and palatable, and make them "feel right" in the mouth. They are very similar in chemical makeup; in fact, the basic difference between an oil and a fat is that a fat is solid at room temperature (e.g., margarine, lard) and an oil is liquid (e.g., corn oil, olive oil). Vegetable oils are oils that are extracted from plants such as corn, soybeans, peanuts, safflower seeds, canola seeds, olives, and sesame seeds. They are available in liquid form or as a cooking spray, in which the oil is combined with lecithin and a propellant, making it easy to apply to cooking and baking pans.

Butter, margarine (and many similar spreads), lard, and shortening are types of fats. They are used as condiments and in baking and cooking. Many processed foods contain shortening.

Most vegetable oils and margarines are made from soybeans, corn, canola, or cottonseed, the four main crops that are genetically modified, as well as often heavily treated with pesticides. Butter is a dairy product and is discussed in chapter 14. Lard is animal fat and should be avoided at all costs. Since pesticides and other toxins accumulate in fat, cooking with lard is essentially like cooking with poison. You may unknowingly eat lard in restaurants that serve Mexican food, as lard is a traditional ingredient in refried beans, tortillas, and other south of the border favorites. You should ask your server in Mexican restaurants if lard is used in their food and avoid those items.

FAT: THE NUTRIENT

The word "fat" also refers to the nutrient that, like carbohydrates and protein, is essential for health and life. When we use the term in this sense, we can talk about different kinds of fat:

- Saturated fats, which are solid at room temperature, such as lard, butter, chicken fat, and coconut and palm "oils" (which are really fats). Saturated fats have long been associated with heart disease, obesity, diabetes, and other conditions.
- Unsaturated fats, which are oils at room temperature. Two fats are in this category: polyunsaturated and monounsaturated fats. Polyunsaturated fats come in two classes: omega-3 and omega-6 fatty acids. Omega-3 fatty acids are beneficial; omega-6 generally are not. Cold-water fish are good sources of the omega-3 fatty acids (see chapter 13). Monounsaturated fats are heart-healthy fats because they lower bad cholesterol (LDL) and raise good

cholesterol (HDL). Olive oil, hempseed oil, flax seed, and flax seed oil are good sources of monounsaturated fats.

- Trans fat, a synthetic byproduct of a chemical process called hydrogenation. Trans fats have recently been identified as being even more detrimental to health than saturated fats. Trans fat is found in many popular processed foods, including potato chips, cereals, salad dressings, baked goods, frozen desserts, frozen dinners, and baking products. These are fats you and your family will want to avoid as much as possible.

CONVENTIONAL OILS

Conventionally prepared oils are those you see most commonly in supermarkets. To make conventional oils, the seeds are crushed at a high temperature (as high as 400 degrees Fahrenheit), which removes some of the oil. Then a solvent, usually hexane (a gasoline-like substance) is added to extract oil from the residue. This process results in up to 95 percent of the oil being extracted from the seeds. The solvent is then removed from the oil using high-temperature steaming. Because it's impossible to remove all the hexane, some of this toxin remains in the oil. This method of making oil is designed to get the most product possible for the least cost, which is why conventional oils are less expensive than cold-pressed varieties, which we discuss below.

Tests conducted in animals show that hexane can cause nervous system problems, Parkinson's-like symptoms (unsteady gait, loss of balance, tremor), and cardiopathy. Two researchers have suggested that solvents like hexane may be associated with the increased occurrence of breast cancer among women. In fact, solvents have been detected in samples of human milk.

Heating and adding solvent during the production process changes the taste of the oil, so the oil needs to be refined and bleached to make it acceptable to consumers. These processes also change the levels of different nutrients, especially vitamin E, sterols (natural plant components that help reduce blood cholesterol levels), and several minerals. Refining can reduce sterol levels by 20 to 60 percent over levels found in cold-pressed oils (see below).

COLD-PRESSED OILS

Cold-pressed oils are healthier than conventionally produced oils. Cold pressing involves placing the seeds in a press at about 50 degrees Fahrenheit. The resulting oil is then filtered, and the oil is stored in a dark container in a cool environment until the sediment settles. Only 30 to 60 percent of the oil can be extracted from seeds using this approach, which is the main reason why cold-pressed oils are more expensive. The residue is fed to farm animals.

Because cold-pressed oils do not undergo heating, treatment with solvents, refining, and bleaching, they retain their nutritional value and don't pick up any toxins in the process. As a bonus, the higher levels of vitamin E in cold-pressed oils allows these oils to go rancid less quickly than conventional oils.

BUYING OILS

When buying oil, keep in mind how much you plan to use within the next few months and how you plan to use it (salad dressing, sautéing, baking) so you'll be sure to purchase the most useful product. You should also become familiar with the following terms, which you will see on different bottles of oil:

- Extra-virgin: This term is used for olive oil only and indicates the best available grade of olive oil. It means that the oil contains less than 1 percent oleic acidity.

- Virgin: When this term is used for olive oil, it means that the oleic acidity level is at 1 to 2 percent. This is the second best grade of olive oil. When "virgin" is used to describe other oils, it means they have not been refined.
- Cold-pressed: This means no external heat was applied while the oil was being extracted and no refining was done after the extraction.
- Pure: A pure oil is one that contains only one type of seed, nut, or fruit. Thus pure corn oil contains oil from corn only.
- Mechanically pressed (also known as expeller-pressed): Any oil that is extracted without the use of solvents is said to be mechanically or expeller-pressed. It does not mean the oil was cold-pressed. In fact, mechanically pressed oils can be processed at a high temperature and refined as well.
- Extra light: This term does *not* mean the oil has less calories; it simply means it has a light taste. If you see these words on a bottle of olive oil and the oil is light in color and taste, it has probably been refined.

GUIDELINES FOR STORING OILS AND FATS

Oils and fats can become rancid rather quickly if they are not stored properly. Rancid fats, besides often tasting terrible, are carcinogenic and have been linked with an increased risk of heart disease and atherosclerosis, so you want to avoid them at all costs.

Three things contribute to a fat going rancid: oxygen (air), light, and heat, with oxygen being the biggest contributor. The more polyunsaturated a fat is, the faster it will turn rancid. The percentages of polyunsaturated fat in common oils are, starting with the highest: safflower (74%), sunflower (66%), corn (60%), soybean (37%), peanut (32%), canola (29%), and olive (8%).

To help prevent your oil from going rancid, follow these guidelines:

- Refrigerate oil, especially once you have opened it. Opened bottles of cooking oils can begin to go rancid within a few weeks or months. It is not always possible to smell rancid oil until it has been so for several months, which is a good reason to always refrigerate opened oil bottles.
- If you buy oil in a plastic container, transfer it to a glass or metal container that you can seal tightly. Transparent containers should be stored in a cool, dark place. Refrigeration is recommended, but a cool cupboard will work as well if you plan to use all the oil within a few weeks.
- Unopened cooking oils typically have a one year shelf life. Some oils, such as sesame and flaxseed, have a shorter life.
- Only buy as much oil as you think you'll use within a few months' time.
- If your refrigerated oil turns cloudy or solid, it will return to its normal clear and liquid form once it reaches room temperature. It is perfectly safe to use it.
- A product that is made of partially hydrogenated vegetable oils and which comes in a solid is hydrogenated shortening (e.g., Crisco, among others). These products are definitely on the "bad" fats list, as hydrogenated and partially hydrogenated oils contribute to heart disease, stroke, and other serious medical conditions. Avoid these products.

USING OILS

Oils can be used in salad dressings or as a seasoning, in baking, or to lightly sauté foods. Yet not every oil is best for each of these uses. Here's a list of various oils and the best ways to use them. Remember to buy cold-pressed oils, organic when possible.

Table 6

Oil	Salads/Seasoning	Bake	Light Sauté
Canola	X	X	
Corn	X	X	
Flaxseed	X		
Hazelnut	X	X	X
Hempseed	X	X	
Olive	X	X	X
Sesame	X	X	X
Soybean	X		
Sunflower	X		
Sweet almond	X	X	X

LET'S GO SHOPPING

Margarine

By law, margarine is at least 80 percent fat, so it is a perfect environment in which toxins can accumulate. The 2001 Total Diet Study found residues of several industrial contaminants in its margarine samples, including chloroform and tetrachloroethylene (probable carcinogens), ethyl benzene, styrene (carcinogen), toluene, and xylene.

You may see margarine products that contain less than 80 percent fat, yet they are still labeled "margarine." Recent labeling regulations by the FDA allow the makers of margarine-type products that are lower than 80 percent fat to sell low-fat and reduced-fat margarines if they are labeled according to FDA guidelines. We have listed these margarine-like products under "Vegetable Oil Spreads."

Safety Hints. The health risks associated with margarine outweigh any possible advantages. In addition to being exposed to industrial chemicals, margarine also is high in unhealthy fats (saturated and trans fats). Healthier alternatives include olive oil for bread and cooking, herbs and lemon for vegetables, and low-fat yogurt for baked potatoes.

If you do buy margarine, you can keep it in the refrigerator for months, or it can be stored in the freezer for up to one year.

Vegetable and Nut Oils

In the Total Diet Study, researchers found residues of benzene, chloroform, endosulfan, styrene, toluene, and xylene in olive/safflower oil samples. Information on other types of vegetable oils is not available. However, vegetable oils can be expected to contain the same pesticide residues as the plants from which they were made. In addition, corn oil and soybean oil, two popular oils in American households, often are made from genetically modified crops, especially in the case of soybeans.

Safety Hints. The healthiest vegetable oils are highest in monounsaturated fat and lowest in saturated fat. Vegetable oils that fit this category include olive oil, flaxseed oil, hempseed oil, and canola oil. (Remember, however, that canola is one of the genetically modified crops, so you may want to look for non-GE canola oil.) The safest oils are organic and cold-pressed; therefore, look for any of the four oils mentioned that are organic and cold-pressed. Some supermarkets carry these items, but you can also find them in natural food stores and food cooperatives (see Appendix also). Store vegetable oils as suggested in the guidelines in this chapter.

Vegetable Oil Spreads

Spreads contain less than 80 percent fat and consist of one or more vegetables oils, at least one of which is usually partially hydrogenated. When oils are hydrogenated, they produce trans fat, a very unhealthy fat that has been linked with heart disease and is, say many experts, even worse for your health than saturated fat.

Vegetable oil spreads can also be expected to contain the same pesticides as the plant from which they were made. In addition, corn oil and soybean oil, which are two of the most common oils found in spreads, often come from genetically modified crops, especially in the case of soybeans.

Vegetable oil spreads may be labeled as such or as reduced-fat, reduced-calorie, diet, light, lower-fat, or fat-free margarine. The FDA has issued criteria for such products. Here's what you're getting when you buy one of these products:

- Reduced-fat, reduced-calorie, or diet margarine: Product contains no more than 60 percent oil, which is a 25 percent reduction in fat and calories over regular margarine (80 percent oil).
- Lower-fat or light margarine: Item contains no more than 40 percent oil (a 50 percent or greater reduction in fat).
- Fat-free margarine: Item contains less than 0.5 gram of fat per serving.

Glossary of Pesticides

2,4-Dichlorophenoxyacetic acid. An herbicide widely used on wheat, rice, and potatoes. Officially it is not a carcinogen, but there is evidence that it can cause birth defects, based on research by Dina Schreinemachers, PhD (*Environmental Health Perspectives*, July 2003). Agent Orange consists of about 50 percent 2,4-D.

Acephate. This organophosphate insecticide is used on brussels sprouts, cauliflower, celery, cranberries, dry beans, lettuce, peanuts, and soybeans. Like all organophosphates, exposure can affect the nervous system and cause nausea, vomiting, shaking, abdominal cramps, sweating, and convulsions. Acephate residues get inside the edible part of the plant and cannot be removed by washing. Cooking, however, does reduce the levels.

Atrazine. The National Resource Defense Council has called for a ban on atrazine from the market, as it has been linked with prostate cancer among workers in atrazine plants. Atrazine is present in the water supply, and thus also can be found in some fish and shellfish, such as shrimp.

Azinphos-methyl. This organophosphate insecticide is applied to berries, grapes, almonds, hazelnuts, pecans, walnuts, pistachios, apples, pears, peaches, melons, cucumbers, eggplant, celery, broccoli, cauliflower, brussels sprouts, cabbage, spinach, potatoes, onions, tomatoes, and snap beans.

Benomyl. Used for mold control, this pesticide was withdrawn from the market by DuPont in 2001, reportedly for economic reasons. Prior to this time, there had been attempts by some groups to ban use of the product, one reason being the possibility that it caused birth defects.

Captan. The EPA has listed this fungicide as a probable human carcinogen. However, it is still used on many crops, including apples and most other fruits, cucumbers, eggplant, beets, celery, broccoli, brussels sprouts, cabbage, cauliflower, collards, kale, lettuce, mustard greens, spinach, potatoes, carrots, onions, turnips, corn, peas, soybeans, and squash (winter and summer).

Carbaryl. This carbamate comes in various formulations, which vary in toxicity from slight to high. It is applied to citrus, other fruits, and nuts. It is considered to be a possible carcinogen. Ingestion can cause nausea, stomach cramps, diarrhea, sweating, blurry vision, and convulsions. Carbaryl is deadly to bees and beneficial insects.

Chlorpyrifos. One of the most commonly used organophosphates in the United States, it is applied to dozens of food crops, including but not limited to cranberries, strawberries, citrus, apples, pears, nectarines, cherries, peaches, plums, grapes, almonds, pecans, walnuts, onions, peppers, kale, broccoli, brussels sprouts, cabbage, cauliflower, collards, asparagus, corn, tomatoes, lentils, beans, peas, wheat, soybeans, peanuts, and bananas. Ingestion can cause nausea, dizziness, confusion, and chest pains.

Chlorpropham. This herbicide is used on lima and snap beans, blueberries, carrots, onions, spinach, tomatoes, soybeans, and garlic, and to inhibit potatoes from sprouting. Long-term exposure may cause tumors.

DDT. Residues of this deadly toxin and its metabolites (breakdown products), DDE and DDD, are still found in the environment, even though DDT has been banned in the United States since 1972. It is, however, still used in some other countries. DDT and its metabolites build up in plants and the fatty tissues of fish and other animals, including humans. Residues are found in meat, fish, and poultry, and some fruits and vegetables. Exposure to DDT can cause seizures and other nervous system problems, as well as premature births in pregnant women.

Diazinon. More than 2 million pounds of this insecticide are used on various agricultural crops and livestock in the United States each year, including rice, fruit, corn, and potatoes. Exposure to diazinon can cause headache, dizziness, weakness, anxiety, nausea and vomiting, diarrhea, abdominal cramps, difficulty breathing, and vision problems. It is highly toxic to fish, birds, and bees. Small amounts are frequently found on foods but the levels are usually below those deemed to cause health problems.

Dicloran. This fungicide is used on carrots, lettuce, peaches, peanuts, potatoes, and tomatoes. High levels given to animals caused liver, kidney, and eye changes. A study in humans showed no ill effects from exposure to dicloran.

Dicofol. Dicofol is used to kill mites, primarily on apples, citrus, strawberries, beans, peppers, tomatoes, and some nuts. It is a possible human carcinogen, as it has caused benign tumors in lab animals.

Dieldrin. Use of this pesticide on crops was banned in the United States in 1974, but it can still be found in the environment. It can build up in the body and affect the nervous system, causing tremors, anxiety, irritability, depression, headache, and dizziness. Residues of dieldrin are found in meat and dairy products, fish and seafood, and in some root crops (e.g., carrots, potatoes, turnips). It is a probable carcinogen.

Endosulfan. This organochlorine is no longer made in the United States, but it is still used (an estimated 1.4 to

2.2 million pounds applied to US crops each year) to help control insects and mites on 60 crops, including pecans, strawberries, and squash. Results of the first human study of the effects of this pesticide were released in December 2003 and showed that exposure to the pesticide damages developing male reproductive hormones and organs. Organochlorines have been linked to nerve damage, Parkinson's disease, various cancers, birth defects, and respiratory illness.

Heptachlor. Use of this pesticide was banned in 1988, but it has lingered for many years in the environment and can still be found in food crops, fish, dairy products, and fatty meats. Exposure to heptachlor can cause dizziness, confusion, and convulsions.

Hexachlorobenzene. This highly toxic pesticide has been banned since 1965, before which it was used to protect seeds of wheat and other grains. However, traces of hexachlorobenzene still remain in the soil and water, and high levels can be found in fish, wheat, and some vegetables, as well as milk and dairy products and meat from cattle that graze in contaminated pastures. The main effect of eating food highly contaminated with hexachlorobenzene is liver disease.

Iprodione. The EPA has listed iprodione as a likely human carcinogen. However, it is still used on apricots, cherries, plums, blueberries, broccoli, kiwi, raspberries, carrots, dry beans, almonds, grapes, garlic, peanuts, lettuce, potatoes, nectarines, and rice.

Lindane. Although this insecticide is listed as a possible carcinogen, it continues to be used on many fruit and vegetable crops in the United States and around the world. Several studies have linked it to breast cancer, and it has been detected in breast milk. Efforts are being made to stop use of this insecticide in North America and Europe. Exposure to lindane is associated with dizziness, seizures, damage to the nervous system, birth defects, and disruption of hormone function.

Malathion. Residues of this commonly used insecticide are among the top ten contaminants found in the FDA's Total Diet Study (16 percent of samples). Especially disturbing is that malathion was detected in 10 percent of infant foods sampled. One metabolite of malathion is more harmful than malathion itself. Symptoms of malathion exposure include difficulty breathing, tight chest, vomiting, abdominal cramps, diarrhea, blurry vision, salivation, sweating, headache, dizziness, and loss of consciousness. It is not listed as a possible or probable carcinogen by the EPA.

Methamidophos. An organophosphate that is used on melons, cucumbers, eggplant, tomatoes, broccoli, brussels sprouts, cabbage, cauliflower, lettuce, and potatoes. There's been no cancer evidence in animals. Methamidophos causes nervous system damage, as well as nausea, vomiting, diarrhea, and cramps. It's been shown to reduce sperm count in humans.

Methoxychlor. This pesticide disrupts the function of hormones, which can cause birth defects, poor short-term memory, attention deficit disorder, cancer, thyroid dysfunction, and low IQ.

Methyl bromide. A fumigant that is injected into the soil before crops are planted. About 60 million pounds of this pesticide are used on more than 120 crops in the United States each year, including grains, rice, spices, broccoli, cauliflower, eggplant, lettuce, onions, tomatoes, citrus, nuts, and many other fruits and vegetables. Because it contributes to ozone layer depletion, methyl bromide is being phased out in developing countries by 2005.

Methyl parathion. One of the most toxic organophosphates, it can overstimulate the nervous system and cause dizziness, nausea, and confusion. Because the acute dietary risk to children ages one to six exceeded the amount that can be safely consumed over a seventy-year lifetime by 880 percent, the EPA requested that farmers voluntarily stop using this pesticide on food crops that are most common in childrens' diets. These foods include all fruits, carrots, succulent peas and beans, and tomatoes. It also is no longer used on artichokes, broccoli, brussels sprouts, cauliflower, celery, collards, kale, kohlrabi, lettuce, mustard greens, rutabaga, spinach, and turnips, but it is still applied to almonds, barley, cabbage, corn, dried beans and peas, lentils, oats, onions, pecans, rice, rye, soybeans, sweet potatoes, walnuts, wheat, and white potatoes.

Permethrin. This pesticide belongs to the group of pyrethroids, and is a possible human carcinogen. Despite this classification, it is used on several crops in the United States, including corn and wheat. Based on tests done on lab animals, children appear to be more sensitive to permethrin than adults. Permethrin can damage DNA and the nervous system and has caused tumors in lab animals.

Thiabendazole. The EPA lists this fungicide as a likely human carcinogen. However, it is still applied to apples, cantaloupe, citrus, dry beans, lentils, mushrooms, pears, potatoes, rice, soybeans, strawberries, sweet potatoes, and other produce. Exposure to thiabendazole can cause dizziness, nausea, vomiting, rash, itching, chills, and headache.

Terbufos. One of the most commonly used organophosphates in the United States (about 7.5 million pounds are applied to crops each year), it is typically applied to corn, sugar beets, and sorghum. Bananas imported from South America have usually been treated with terbufos, but the insecticide is not used on bananas grown in the United States. The EPA reports that consumers should not be concerned about experiencing ill effects from exposure to terbufos on food.

Toxaphene. This organochlorine was banned in the United States in 1990, yet it remains in the environment. Residues accumulate in mammals and fish, and it is often detected in shellfish as well. It may be carcinogenic; however, there is little information on its effect in humans.

Avoiding Foodborne Illness

How to Avoid Foodborne Diseases

- Make grocery shopping the last thing you do before returning home to minimize the time the food stays unrefrigerated. If necessary, bring a cooler and several ice packs in your car so you can place refrigerated items in the cooler.
- Do not purchase canned items that have been dented or otherwise damaged.
- If you purchase packaged meat, poultry, or fish, juices from these items may leak onto other grocery items. Therefore, these items should be placed in individual plastic bags at the meat or checkout counter.
- Refrigerate all perishable items as soon as you get home.
- Regularly check your refrigerator and freezer temperatures: The refrigerator temperature should be between 40 and 42° F and the freezer should be at 0° F.
- Refrigerate all sauces and dressings such as ketchup, salad dressings, and mayonnaise after you open them.

- Do not keep highly perishable products in the door panel of the refrigerator because this is the warmest part of the appliance.
- Regularly rotate the items in your cupboards to make sure you are using the oldest items first. Generally it is safest to dispose of items that are past their expiration date (see "How to Read Dated Food Labels" below).
- Wash your hands thoroughly before preparing food. This means using soap and warm water for twenty to thirty seconds and then drying your hands with a clean towel.
- If you are handling raw meat, poultry, or fish, never allow these foods or the utensils they touch to come in contact with any other food items. Always wash your hands thoroughly before and after handling these raw foods.
- Do not consume raw eggs or any food that includes raw eggs, such as some homemade ice creams or salad dressings. Do not eat raw cake batter or cookie dough that contains raw eggs.
- When defrosting foods, do so overnight in the refrigerator or in a microwave. Do not leave frozen items out on the counter to thaw.
- Keep counters clean with soap and warm water, and sanitize them regularly with a solution containing two teaspoons of bleach in 32 ounces of water.

How to Read Dated Food Labels

- Expiration dates, such as "Expires 1/15/05" or "Do not use after 5/30/06" are generally seen on certain boxed and bottled items, vitamins, infant formulas, and sensitive products such as yeast. Generally, it is best to dispose of items that have gone past their expiration date. Vitamins, for example, will be less effective, and yeast may not work.
- Pack dates, which are usually in code, tell when items were packaged. Pack dates are typically used

on canned foods, boxed cookies and crackers, cereals, and spices. Usually these items maintain their quality for at least twelve to eighteen months after their pack date.

- "Sell by" dates (also called "pull dates") are usually seen on refrigerated items, such as milk, cream, luncheon meats, eggs, yogurt, and cheese. These dates mean the store must remove the items from the shelf by the date listed. If the food has been properly refrigerated, it is safe to eat for up to seven days after the "sell by" date. However, if you notice a bad smell, the seal is broken, or there is mold or discoloration on the food, throw it out.

- Quality dates, or "Better if used by" dates, are often found on cold cereals, baby food, peanut butter, and packaged mixes. These dates mean that the food item will lose its good flavor and may begin to taste "off" if consumed after the listed date. These dates are estimates; an item that says "Better if used by May 1, 2005" will not suddenly taste bad on May 2, 2005. It is best to dispose of baby food that is past the quality date; other items such as cereals or peanut butter may still be eaten, but you may notice some change in quality.

How to Report Adverse Reactions to Foods

The Food and Drug Administration's Center for Food Safety and Applied Nutrition developed the Adverse Reaction Monitoring System (ARMS) to analyze consumer complaints about food additives. To report an adverse reaction, go to www.fda.gov/opacom/backgrounders/problem.html and scroll down to "How do I report nonemergencies about food?" and click on DISTRICT OFFICE CONSUMER COMPLAINT COORDINATOR to get the number for your area. If it is an emergency, call 301-443-1240. For both emergencies and nonemergencies, you should have the following information available:

- Give names, addresses, and phone numbers of persons affected. Include your name, address, and phone number, as well as that of the doctor or hospital if emergency treatment was provided.
- Describe the food item as completely as possible, including any codes or identifying marks on the label or container. Give the name and address of the store where the product was purchased and the date of purchase.
- You also should report the problem to the manufacturer or distributor shown on the label and to the store where you purchased the product.

Resources

FOOD SUPPLIERS

Organic and Non-GM Oils

Catania
1 Nemco Way, PO Box J, Ayer MA 01432
800-343-5522
www.cataniausa.com
Organic and non-GM oils

Spectrum Naturals/Spectrum Organic Products
5341 Old Redwood Highway, Suite 400, Petaluma CA 94954
www.spectrumnaturals.com/products.html
Organic and non-GM oils

Sun Organic Farm
411 S. Las Posas Road, San Marcos CA 92069
888-269-9888
www.sunorganicfarm.com

Whole Foods Market
601 N. Lamar, Suite 300, Austin TX 18703
512-477-4455
www.wholefoods.com/products/365organic
365 Organic Everyday Value brand, available in Whole
Foods stores

Organic and/or Whole Grains, Beans, Etc.

Amwell Valley Organic Grains
PO Box 411, Ringoes NJ 08551
www.farmersteve.com
Organic popcorn

Arrowhead Mills
734 Franklin Avenue, #444, Garden City NY 11530
800-434-4246
www.arrowheadmills.com
Organic whole grain flours, baking and pancake mixes,
cereals, nut butters   •

Bob's Red Mill
5209 SE International Way, Milwaukie OR 97222
800-379-2173
www.bobsredmill.com
Organic whole grains

Eden Foods
701 Tecumseh Road, Clinton MI 49236
888-441-3336
www.edenfoods.com
Beans, condiments, fruits, juices, oils and vinegars, pastas, snacks, soymilk

Fantastic Foods
www.fantasticfoods.com
Cereals, ready meals, soups, pastas, side dishes

Hain-Celestial Company
Consumer Affairs, 4600 Sleepytime Drive, Boulder CO
80301
800-434-4246

www.hain-celestial.com
Makers of Hain Pure Foods (crackers, cookies, snacks, oils); Westbrae (meals, vegetables, whole grains, beans, soups); Westsoy (soy beverages); Health Valley (soups, cereals, baked goods); Imagine Foods (nondairy beverages, soups, frozen desserts); Yves Veggie Cuisine (meat and cheese alternatives); Casbah (mixes and side dishes), Garden of Eatin' (snack chips); Earth Best (organic non-GMO baby foods)

Lightlife
153 Industrial Boulevard, Turners Falls MA 01376
800-SOY-EASY
www.lightlife.com
Vegetarian bacon, beef, chicken, hot dogs, meatballs, etc.

Nasoya
One New England Way, Ayer MA 01432
800-VITASOY
www.vitasoy-usa.com/nasoya
Marinated and plain tofu, seasoning mixes, pasta, dressings, wrappers

Nature's Path
888-808-9505
www.naturespath.com
Bars, breads, cereals, waffles

Veggie Patch
FoodTech International Inc., 26 Kendall Street, New Haven CT 06612
www.veggiepatch.com
Variety of soy-based "meats"

Walnut Acres
4600 Sleepytime Drive, Boulder CO 80301
866-492-5688
www.walnutacres.com
Juices, salsas, sauces, snacks, soups

Organic Meat and Dairy Products

Horizon Organic
PO Box 17577, Boulder CO 80308-7577
888-494-3020
www.horizonorganic.com
Organic milk, yogurt, butter, pudding, eggnog, sour
cream, eggs, juices, cottage cheese, cheese

Organic Valley
www.organicvalley.com
Organic milk, cheese, eggs, butter, juices, meat

Stonyfield Farm
Ten Burton Drive, Londonderry NH 03053
800-PRO-COWS
www.stonyfield.com/HealthyFood/index.shtml
Organic yogurt, milk, smoothies, ice cream, frozen yogurt

Willow Hill Farm
Milton, VT
802-893-2963
www.sheepcheese.com
Organic sheep's milk, cheese, and yogurt; grass-fed lamb;
organic cow's milk and cheese

Organic Wine

Frey Vineyards
14000 Tomki Road, Redwood Valley CA 94470
800-760-3739
www.freywine.com

Organic Wine Company
888-326-9463
www.organicconsumers.org/sponsors/ecowine

INFORMATION SOURCES

Foodborne Illness and Food Alerts

National Institutes of Health
www.niaid.nih.gov/factsheets/foodbornedis.htm

Safety Alerts
www.safetyalerts.com/what_is.htm
Free e-mail service that alerts you to product recalls in 16
categories (one is food) as they occur. Choose as many or
as few categories as you wish.

United States Department of Agriculture
www.fsis.usda.gov/OA/recalls/rec_intr.htm

Genetically Modified Foods

The Campaign to Label Genetically Engineered Foods
PO Box 55699, Seattle WA 98155
425-771-4049
www.thecampaign.org

The Genetically Engineered Food Alert Campaign
Center
1200 18th Street, NW, 5th Floor, Washington DC 20036
800-390-3373
www.gefoodalert.org

Mothers for Natural Law
PO Box 1177, Fairfield IA 52556
800-REALFOOD
www.safe-food.org

Pesticide Action Network North America (PANNA)
www.panna.org/campaigns/ge.html

General Food Safety and Health

Center for Food Safety
www.centerforfoodsafety.org
Protects human health and the environment by curbing
harmful food production practices and promoting organic
and other sustainable agriculture

The Center for Food Safety and Applied Nutrition of
the Food and Drug Administration (CFSAN)

800-FDA-4010
http://vm.cfsan.fda.gov

The Food and Nutrition Information Center
301-504-5719
www.nal.usda.gov/fnic

National Environmental Trust
1200 18th Street, NW, 5th Floor, Washington DC 20036
202-887-8800
www.net.org
Nonprofit, nonpartisan organization established to inform citizens about environmental problems and how they affect health

The National Food Safety Database
www.foodsafety.org

Irradiation

Foundation for Food Irradiation Education
www.food-irradiation.com

Public Citizen
1600 20th Street NW, Washington DC 20009
202-588-1000
www.citizen.org/cmep/foodsafety/food_irrad
National nonprofit public interest group, promotes a sustainable future

Stop Food Irradiation Project
http://organicconsumer.org/irradlink.html

Organic Foods and Agriculture

California Certified Organic Farmers
1115 Mission Street, Santa Cruz CA 95060
888-423-2263
www.ccof.org

Local Harvest
www.localharvest.org
Helps consumers find organic produce in their area

Organic Consumers Association
6101 Cliff Estate Road, Little Marais MN 55614
218-226-4164
www.organicconsumers.org
Campaign for food safety, organic agriculture, fair trade,
and sustainability

Organic Farming Research Foundation
PO Box 440, Santa Cruz CA 95061
831-426-6606
www.ofrf.org
Information on organic agriculture

The Organic Trade Association
www.theorganicreport.org
"Organic information and inspiration"

Pesticides

Pesticide Action Network North America (PANNA)
www.panna.org

Pesticide Action Network International
www.pan-international.org

Pesticide Education Center
www.pesticides.org/educmaterials.html

Organic Farming Research Foundation
www.ofrf.org
Learn about alternatives to pesticide use

Natural Resources Defense Council
www.nrdc.org
Learn about effects of pesticides on health, environment

Environmental Working Group
www.ewg.org
Learn about effects of pesticides on health, environment

Physicians for Social Responsibility
www.envirohealthaction.org/bearingtheburden
Learn about effects of pesticides on health

Our Stolen Future
www.ourstolenfuture.org
Learn about effects of pesticides on health

Collaborative on Health and the Environment
www.cheforhealth.org
Learn about effects of pesticides on health, environment

SUGGESTED READING

CQ Researcher. *On Saving the Environment*. Washington DC: CQ Press, 2001.

Hart, Kathleen. *Eating in the Dark: America's Experiment with Genetically Engineered Food*. New York: Pantheon Books, 2002.

Leon, Warren, and Caroline DeWaal. *Is Our Food Safe: A Consumer's Guide to Protecting Your Health and the Environment*. Three Rivers Press, 2002.

Nestle, Marion. *Food Politics: How the Food Industry Influences Nutrition and Health*. Berkeley: University of California Press, 2002.

Nestle, Marion. *Safe Food: Bacteria, Biotechnology, and Bioterrorism*. Berkeley: University of California Press, 2003.

Renders, Eileen, ND. *Food Additives, Nutrients & Supplements A to Z*. Santa Fe: Clear Light Publishers, 1999.

Roberts, Cynthia. *The Food Safety Information Handbook*. Westport CT: Oryx Press, 2001.

Satin, Morton. *Food Alert! The Ultimate Sourcebook for Food Safety*. New York: Facts on File Inc., 1999.

Simontacchi, Carol. *The Crazy Makers: How the Food Industry Is Destroying Our Minds and Harming Our Children*. New York: Jeremy P. Tarcher/Putnam, 2000.

Smith, Jeffrey. *Seeds of Deception: Exposing Industry and Government Lies about the Safety of the Genetically Engineered Foods You Are Eating*. White River Junction VT: Chelsea Green Publishing Company, 2003.